BUSINESS MADE SIMPLE;

The Journey To Simple Passive Cash Flow

Jamie Louis

Copyright © 2022 by Jamie P.louis.All Right Reserved.

No part of this publication may be reproduced, distributed,or transmitted in any form or by any means, including photocopying,recording,or other electronic or mechanical methods,or by any information storage and retrieval system without permissions of the author, except in the case of very brief quotation embodied in critical reviews and certain other non-commercial uses permitted by copyright

This book's author, Jamie P. Louis, is an expert in relationships, health, and parenting. Great Experience. Great Value.

Enjoy a great reading experience with the Kindle edition of this book. Learn more about Great on Kindle, available in select categories.

Also books like:

OBESITY CODE AND MANAGEMENT

METHOD TO PARENTING TEENS

OBESITY ANTIDOTE IN MODERN WORLD

MANAGEMENT OF PARENTING KIDS WITH ADHD IN MODERN ERA

THE WONDERFUL BOOK ON PERFECT MARRIAGE

Please Don't Forget To Drop Your Review

Table of contents

Chapter 1

Chapter 2

Chapter 3

Table of contents

Chapter 1

Selling Yourself And Your Products To Others

(I) Developing Positive Attitude

(II) Building Self Confidence And Risk Taking Courage

(III) The Power Of Listening Ears, Enthusiasm And Body Language In Business

Chapter 2

The Secret Of Good Salesmanship And Leadership In Business

(I) Time Management And Expenditure

(II) The Secret Of Winning Clients And Accumulation Of Market Power

(III) The Strategy Of Closing A Sales

(IV) Learning From Competitors And Boost Sales

Chapter 3

Affiliate Marketing

(I) Fundamentals And Benefits Of Social Media Marketing
(I) Social Strategies
(II) Facebook And Instagram Marketing

(III) YouTube, TikTok And Twitter Marketing
(III) Email And Website Marketing

(II) Digital Marketing Sale Funnel
(I) Building A Sale Funnel For Your Business
(II) Business Traffic

(III) Branding
(I) Increase Brand Awareness

Chapter 1

Selling Yourself And Your Products To Others

When purchasing expensive capital goods, the buyer is making a long-term commitment to you and your business, not just purchasing a commodity. They risk losing their jobs if the product doesn't work. So much more than the qualities and advantages of the profits are involved in successful selling. The salesperson must establish a long-lasting, trust-based relationship.Promote your firm, yourself, and eventually your product.

When purchasing expensive capital goods, the consumer is not just making a one-time purchase; rather, they are committing to working with you and your business for the foreseeable future. They risk losing their jobs if the product doesn't work. So much more than the features and advantages of the profits are involved in successful selling. The salesperson must establish a long-lasting, trust-based relationship. You can only achieve that by establishing your own credibility first, before requesting the customer to put their trust in your business. Repeated application of this adage will benefit you throughout your career.

You might now believe that if your product is excellent, customers will buy it based solely on that fact.

Note;"Your product needs to be outstanding because otherwise, you won't get in the door." A fantastic product is only the beginning, as a customer's company and career are in greater danger the more money they spend with you. The semiconductor industry is full of manufacturers and products that at first glance seemed great but ultimately fell short.

That's great! This will provide you the chance to examine all of our goods and business advantages side by side, including any that you might be taking for granted.

There is no end point to marketing. It's a process that is constantly changing. The rise and collapse of different marketing methods and campaigns have captivated the world over the years. The key to a successful brand can be a strong marketing plan.

(I) Developing Positive Attitude

A positive mindset is the foundation of a successful sales career. A positive mindset is the foundation of a successful sales career. Your shared attitude sets the tone for daily interactions with coworkers, clients, prospects, and management. The people you deal with will want to keep working with you if you have a positive attitude, which will increase your sales success overall.

Here are a few instances that illustrate how crucial having a positive attitude is in sales.

Recognizing that a person's attitude is a matter of personal choice is crucial. This indicates that you have the power to decide to have a positive attitude, not other people or things. Your stress levels will start to drop once you realize that you have the capacity to positively affect sales by deliberately choosing to have a fantastic attitude about your profession. This is because having a happy attitude alters your perception. Overall, this makes it simpler to organize your workload, set priorities, and pay attention to the actually crucial sales activities you must complete, further reducing the impact of stress.

Although it may sometimes be true, the adage "opposites attract" is untrue when it comes to attitudes! Think about this Would you prefer to be among individuals who are exhibiting negativity or people who are in a happy mood when something wonderful has happened to you during the day? A positive sales approach attracts others, which is crucial when trying to persuade potential customers and clients. It is much simpler to close sales when you have a positive mindset and your prospects and clients are responding similarly.

Your career depends on the growth of your sales. By making it simpler for you to accept the learning opportunities you find along the route, a positive attitude enables you to achieve success in sales as well as on a personal level. If you embrace these chances to try new things and learn new strategies positively, you will be better able to create beneficial, long-lasting improvements that increase your sales. Additionally, your terrific attitude, which people with whom you work notice and admire, may encourage your advancement to positions of higher responsibility. Growth in sales through learning via good reactions to situations can also help you do this.

Being positive makes it easier to complete challenging tasks.

It might require a lot of work to resolve customer difficulties and get over obstacles, but this does not mean that these duties must be unpleasant. Instead, if you have a positive outlook even in the face of challenging situations, you may convert such situations into success stories by striving for the best result for all parties involved. Instead of avoiding problems, you may empower yourself to handle them head-on and improve your sales connections by adopting a positive mindset.

(II) You can manage your sales outcomes when you are optimistic.

How would it feel to have total control over your sales results? You are, in fact, especially if you have a positive mindset. Social scientists and psychologists have frequently discussed the effects of the "self-fulfilling prophecy." Your sales will move in the direction you intend if you approach your activities with a positive attitude, feel that you can accomplish your goals, and take the necessary efforts to make sure that they are realized.

A positive attitude may affect, support, and grow your sales in a variety of other ways. However, seeing the best sales performers and sales executives you most respect may be the simplest approach to understanding the impact that a positive attitude has on sales. You can get the same outcomes for yourself if you adopt the positive mindsets that these salespeople do.

95 percent of sales success is mental. In the end, you will be correct if you don't believe you can be successful or get a transaction. The ability to stay upbeat, though, gives you a significant competitive edge.

The sales industry is an extremely difficult one to work in nowadays. Numerous sales representatives contend with impossibly tight timelines, severe accountability, hundreds of curveballs with each contract, and pipeline scrutiny from all angles as a result of the ongoing changes in how firms sell.However, there is a hidden weapon:
Optimism.
Every sales performer needs a positive approach, and it's one of the things that has made me successful. Are you wondering how you can be optimistic when you and your team have two days remaining in the month and are just 48 percent complete with the plan?

Experience taught me that maintaining a happy attitude was important for my sales success, for my family (who occasionally grumble that my optimism is downright irritating), as well as for my prospects, customers, coworkers, and community.

Maintaining a positive attitude mostly depends on one's perspective and thinking. It all depends on the perspective you use to view your work, your daily responsibilities, and your career.

Recognize what you might have done better, then move on. Of course, it takes experience to achieve this, but having this attitude will pay you in the long term.

Knowing why you do what you do helps you concentrate on your objectives while riding through the ups and downs that come with working in sales. I'm motivated by my love of my profession, my faith in our brand and mission, and the fantastic team I work with."

To maintain your optimism, keep in mind that you are not a number. Your quota is not a reflection of your work, care, or ideals."If anything is wrong, try to remedy it if you can, but learn to stop worrying; worrying never solves problems."

That also entails being kind to yourself and accepting that you will have some difficult periods. Use the following tactics to help you stay optimistic when times are difficult.

1. Clearly state your annual goals in writing.
In essence, beneficial best practices for salespeople at all levels include maintaining your goals front and center and planning for difficulties before they emerge.

Make a vision board, This is a great method to keep your top priorities in mind. A vision board is a collection of images that represent your goals and desires for your profession and/or personal life. It can be digital or real. This may involve substantial expenditures, trip locations, or significant achievements.

You'll discover that by imagining it and acting out the worst-case scenario, you may develop a better plan of action to get out of that challenging position, and stay more grounded and upbeat as a result."Your vision board should inspire you to let the little things go and keep you moving on the right path.

2. Possess a solid basis.
You should not take your health for granted. The three pillars of performance, are eating well, getting adequate sleep, and exercising. These are essential activities that might support you in maintaining a good outlook in a hard profession like sales.

When salesmen get irritable or show signs of burnout, it may be time to take a break and put more of an emphasis on taking care of oneself.

3. Increase your use of humor throughout the day.
Find a clever pun, joke,or sales phrase that will amuse you and the people you interact with. You might feel happier if you can laugh at yourself or use suitable humor to start a conversation.

If you don't feel comfortable sharing jokes, consider adding your favorite comedian's stand-up to your playlist to help you stay upbeat throughout the day.

4.Consider all of your errors, especially the major ones, as teaching opportunities.
Even though they can be upsetting and expensive, errors are a part of life that we can learn from. I occasionally encourage sales representatives to name the three errors they commit most frequently so they can remember them, not become fixated on them, and understand that making errors is a necessary part of learning how to become a better salesman.

5. Keep in mind that you are offering a service.
In the end, the purpose of your business is to meet the demands of your clients.Focus on the advantages of your business and the goods you offer.

"Sometimes we put in the same amount of effort and may wind up on the wrong side of luck. Other times, we land on the right side of luck and have large months or great years. The important thing is to keep going, act morally, and take charge of what we can.

You must have faith in both the process and in yourself. Avoid being excessively elated or too dejected. Ride those highs and be ready to press the brakes when necessary. Just keep going; have faith in your abilities and the process."

(II) Building Self Confidence And Risk
Being confident is a crucial talent that may be developed through practice. The transmission of confidence is the key to sales. You are giving the customer a message that you are confident in your solution and that you are the best choice. I frequently wonder how you expect the consumer to believe you are the best option if you can't even persuade yourself of that.

Therefore, the first step is to see yourself as the consumer.Understanding their viewpoint and suffering can help you connect with them more easily, boost their confidence, and know how to best assist them.

The quote "If there's one key to success, it rests in the capacity to get to the other person's point of view and understand things from that person's standpoint as well as from your own" Well, I wholeheartedly concur. You'll be better able to approach the situation with confidence and win their trust and confidence the more you can comprehend their point of view before attempting to address the problem or issue at hand.

The second point is about being aware of the special contribution you make.
In a sales situation, you must put in a lot of effort to comprehend the customer's problem before figuring out how you can address it specially.

What distinguishing features do you offer in your solution? How can you reframe or reinvent the problem in ways that the opposition may not have done, and how can you present and present the problem in a way that shows the value you are bringing?

The more you can approach a customer and say, "You know, that reminds me of a circumstance, exactly like yours, that we recently had and a situation that came out with a really happy finish, or that provided a lot of value for the business," the more successful you will be. In order to enable the client and yourself, to feel more confident while discussing your goods and solutions, it is important to know which of our tales are the most comparable to or relevant to their scenario.

I'll add being an expert as the fourth point.
Take the time to thoroughly research your industry, solution, and product so that you can establish yourself as an authority on the subject. You can't be expected to know all there is to know about the solution, so go the extra mile and read the supplementary information,

conduct internet research, subscribe to the blogs, download the white papers, or find other materials that will help you get new insights.

And instead of having to defend your approach, make up a solution, or be unable to respond to a question, you may speak to them from a position of power and competence. So, be knowledgeable and enquiring.

Don't be desperate is the last point I'll make. It might be challenging if you're attempting to close that transaction and you could come out as being overly eager, receptive, or even frantic to take advantage of the chance. That makes us lose faith in you. In that circumstance, we are lagging behind.

The only way to respond to it is to keep your funnel full, to prospect, to take advantage of more chances, and to go out and consider all of the potential pursuits and opportunities that are out there. So that you won't be frantically trying to close one if it starts to drag or go sideways since you have others that will keep your pipeline filled and keep you working.

Finally, you may say to the customer, "Oh, that's wonderful. When you're ready, we'll meet (but make sure you get a commitment to a subsequent step)." If you put pressure on them like you need to finish a contract this week, it will come out as desperate, which will damage your confidence.

You'll come across as much more confident, win the customer's trust, and have a higher chance of closing the deal if you can keep those things in mind as you enter a deal: comprehend their viewpoint, offer a special solution, offer that expertise that will differentiate you from the competition, tell your story, and avoid being desperate to close the deal.

In sales, confidence is crucial. A salesperson who lacks self-assurance is comparable to a lawyer who lacks drive. However, confidence doesn't come naturally when you have to deal with rejection from prospects regularly.

Contrary to popular belief, you may boost your confidence by using a few easy tips and life hacks. If they work in sales and want to earn more money. They should also apply the following advice to increase their confidence and complete more deals:

1. Be ready.
One of the finest methods to boost your confidence is to put in the effort to prepare for a presentation. There won't be anything to worry about when it comes to doing your duties effectively if you are well familiar with both your goods and your pitch.

2. Speak forcefully
It doesn't matter what I say, as long as I say it with intonation, Blues Traveler once sung. Not far from the truth is this. You'll feel more certain and assertive when

you speak in that manner. More importantly, your client will react appropriately.

3. Promote a product you adore.
Having confidence in what you're selling will come effortlessly if you genuinely believe in it. All you need to do is properly convey the word that the product is valuable to your clients and of excellent quality. You already have faith in it.

4. Modify your stance
According to studies, you may increase your confidence by altering your body language. Even better, clients will react appropriately to your body language. Puff out your chest and stand tall before a pitch; it will assist.

5. Workout
Exercise is the solution to bad health, which destroys confidence. You don't have to train like an amateur bodybuilder to reap the benefits of regular exercise for your life and, more significantly, your sales profession.

6. Avoid being negative
Without the negative stuff that you find at nearly every organization, selling is challenging enough. Avoid them at all costs since, even though moping about may be soothing, it destroys confidence.

7. Consider your accomplishments
When you're feeling down, it could be helpful to reflect on your successes, particularly those that were very

significant to you. When you feel you need inspiration the most, write down a few of the things you're most proud of and refer to them.

Risk Taking

You are far more inclined to take chances if you are highly motivated by sales. You're more likely to be successful in sales if you're more ready to take chances. The only things that will have changed in your life in ten years, are the books you've read and the people you've met. The more I think about it, the more I see how accurate it is. I would even add one more qualification to it: after ten years, your life will have changed about changes you have made. Too many individuals avoid taking chances. They believe that danger is a negative thing for whatever reason. But I've discovered that the more chances you take, the more at ease you get with them. How can we possibly believe that our sales motivation will be as high as it can be if we're not prepared to take chances?

I've discovered that a person's degree of sales motivation directly relates to the amount of risk they are prepared to take. People will take more risk when they are more driven, and less risk when they are less motivated. Success comes to those who go forward rather than those who wait around. Yes, taking a risk does not always translate into success, but you are far more likely to succeed if you try. Additionally, trying implies taking a chance as opposed to remaining passive.

- How can I raise the amount of risk I take? I ask myself.
- How can I push my sales process in fresh ways to achieve even greater success?

I am more driven when I push my comfort zone with danger. I'm more driven to take on additional risk as a result of my increased sales incentive. Who are you? What are your thoughts on risk? And in 2010, are you going to take more? It could affect how motivated you are to sell!

One characteristic you'll see among the most prosperous businesspeople of our day is that they take risks.

The story of inventor James Dyson is one of my favorites about a risk-taker. "The secret to success is failure," he has declared. Ninety-nine percent of success is failure.

He talks from his experience. Dyson really failed 5,127 times. You read correctly. Before he was successful, he created 5,127 vacuum cleaner prototypes. Describe your grit. Obviously, this is an extreme case. However, Dyson's tenacity paid off. He is estimated to be worth $7.7 billion as of 2022.

Risk management is a topic that comes up regularly in our interactions.

Given some of their sectors, it makes sense to respond in this way. But if salespeople don't take any risks and instead try to reduce their fear of making errors, what are the costs in terms of talent, learning, creativity, and sales results? Do you think that part of your sales training should cover taking calculated risks?

Of course, there is a continuum of risk, and it pays to increase our understanding of which risks are wise and which ones might result in significant long-term harm. The following suggestions can help you and your sales team succeed by taking calculated risks:
Make a sincere evaluation of the situation. Examine your organization's risk tolerance after researching your sector as a whole. In regard to the sector, evaluate how your culture differs. Repeat the process for your functional area, your team, and finally yourself. It's critical to understand how you rank organizationally and which employees are most prone to take risks and make errors. Here are a couple queries to get you going:

- Which businesses in my sector appear to be forging new ground with innovative goods, services, or procedures?
- What are the conclusions?
- What characteristics do those who are causing that have?
- What attitudes and abilities do they possess?
- What function did growth and learning serve?
- How do my mentality, abilities, and accomplishments compare to those of those sales people?

Assess the risk associated with your sales training. There are several ways to approach this, in terms of both design and content. You may evaluate yourself as a sales leader or training leader by asking the following questions:

- Are the members of my sales team able to quickly leave their comfort zones and adopt new viewpoints?
- Are the members of my sales team learning to take calculated risks and make mistakes?
- Do they present fresh concepts to potential customers and clients?

Give it a structure. Contrary to popular belief, a little structure might make people feel more comfortable taking risks. Consider failure and errors from a different angle. Because we live in a culture that values outcomes above all else, the majority of us have been trained to view errors and failures negatively. Additionally, errors might reduce the bottom line in sales. But what if we, as sales leaders, adopted a different perspective on errors, rewarding risk-taking and hard work before results? Making errors and taking calculated risks are just growth opportunities.

People are inspired to try again when we take the time to appreciate their efforts and remove any criticism. Mistakes might be viewed as "stepping stones" to the intended result rather than as "failures" that must be rectified. Your team might become more open, optimistic, devoted, and creative with this new perspective.

What have you discovered about risk-taking and failure? And are you prepared to assist your sales team in taking calculated risks?
Read my essay on cultivating a growth attitude for further advice on building resilience in your sales team.

(III)The Power Of Listening Ears, Enthusiasm And Body Language In Business

Salespeople find it more challenging to prove their knowledge as a result. Additionally, it becomes more challenging to create credibility and finally develop trust if they are unable to show knowledge. Without credibility and trust, a salesman is likely to lose their prospect's attention or, worse still, never truly capture it.

What therefore ought salespeople to do? Simple: Make listening a priority. Reps who don't listen lose the chance to establish rapport, identify the wants of the buyer, and demonstrate to the prospect that you are aware of their concerns.

The problem is that listening may be quite challenging. Too frequently, salespeople don't actually listen to the prospect; instead, they wait their turn to speak or plan their next move. I've taught the representatives who have reported to me throughout the years a very particular skill: active listening, in order to get rid of this behavior.

Some would contend that the effectiveness of a salesperson's active listening abilities directly correlates with their earning potential. One of the finest perfections we may achieve in the art of selling is the ability to listen intently and respond effectively. "To listen well is as potent a method of persuasion as to talk well,". While everyone may gain from this wise counsel, experienced sellers should pay particular attention to it. No salesperson has ever talked themselves out of making a deal.

The physical process of hearing and the emotional skill of listening are commonly confused by bad listeners. Although the hearing is a biological ability, active listening abilities must be learned and refined. When you talk throughout the selling process, you only supply information; however, when you listen, you demonstrate respect, foster trust, and establish rapport. Unfortunately, speaking and writing are highly valued in today's educational institutions, but active listening is not. For instance, there are many intelligent people with high academic honors who are proficient in several languages but who are utterly incapable of listening. The good news is that you can always work on honing your active listening techniques, whether it's at the dinner table or the sales counter.

Making a deliberate effort to hear your customer out as well as to attempt to comprehend the full information being given, both orally and nonverbally, is known as active listening. You have to use both of your senses when listening—your eyes as well as your ears. Keep an eye out for consistency between your customer's words, posture, movement, and tone of voice as well as their body language signals.

Are you able to maintain your attention on your consumer, or does it occasionally stray? Giving your consumer your complete and undivided attention not only demonstrates respect but also helps establish connections and builds trust. Put distractions aside and train your mind to focus. Every time you see your thoughts beginning to stray, "grab it" and bring them back to your consumer.

The most effective marketers tend to listen like homicide detectives and offer excellent probing questions to better understand and encourage discourse. They summarize and seek clarification rather than making assumptions. It shows that you understood the message when you ask a question or make a comment to summarize what was spoken. Your consumer will fight against your suggestions until this is done.

Consider including the following active listening suggestions in your sales presentation if you want to increase the efficacy of your sales efforts.

- Give your consumer your full and undivided attention by facing them.
- By sitting up straight, maintaining clear eye contact, uncrossing your legs, spreading your arms, and leaning slightly forward, you may convey your attention through your body language.
- Cut down on distractions by putting your phone off.
- By nodding your head in agreement, you should respond correctly to demonstrate that you understand.
- Use open-ended inquiries to urge your client to provide more details, such as "How did you feel when that happened?"
- Keep an open mind, and don't interrupt.
- Clarification-seeking queries and frequent comment summaries are appropriate. To make sure you didn't get your customer's point of view wrong, rephrase their main points. Begin by saying, "So, if I understand you right, you're saying…

Where there is inadequate communication, errors proliferate, relationships fall apart, and sales chances are lost! I strongly advise you to listen as you work if you want to boost your sales performance, relationships, and professional image.

Enthusiasm

You won't be able to obtain real accomplishments in sales until you comprehend how excitement impacts your outcomes. Sales are about assisting others and persuading them to realize the benefits of doing business with you. Once you've done that, it will help in persuading people to act. This is why having optimism for the future is necessary if you want to influence.

"Enthusiasm is a state of mind that motivates and encourages one to carry out the work at hand. Enthusiasm is the crucial propelling energy that propels activity, bearing a similar relationship to a human as steam does to a locomotive. Through Napoleon Hill.Energy is passion. Energy may be transported, as you may know, but it cannot be destroyed. This is why having energy is crucial if you want to gain influence. The customer feels your energy as you infuse them with optimism for the future. You need to trust and have faith in what you can provide the customer through the goods you are selling if you want to have greater energy. Your primary goal needs to be that. Always think about what you can do for your client. "How can I make it better for them?" Be enthusiastic about how you can provide them with a better future.

What do excitement and fuel have in common?

They both provide us with the motivation to move onward. Gasoline is ignited in an engine to produce the power needed to move our cars. Similar to how excitement, when appropriately sparked, propels us ahead in life, career, and relationships.

The best indicator of successful sales is enthusiasm. Enthusiasm will always win out over any other quality in me. Hard effort, skill, and intelligence alone are not as valuable. Add some zeal, and you've got a powerful combination! Greatness is bred through enthusiasm. Consider the people you know who have achieved remarkable things as an illustration. Most likely, they all possess a passionate zest for what they do.

"One of the most potent success motors is enthusiasm. Put your all into whatever you do. Put all of your heart into it. Add your unique personality to it. By being active, energizing, passionate, and devoted, you may achieve your goal. Without enthusiasm, nothing spectacular has ever been accomplished.

Enthusiasm should not be confused with excitement. When you witness a walk-off home run in the bottom of the ninth inning, excitement fills the stadium. The inner urge you have when you want to play baseball is enthusiasm. Enthusiasm is just enthusiasm that has been amplified by inspiration, motivation, and tenacity.

The ability to be enthusiastic may propel you to achievement. Additionally, it fuels the physical body. Salespeople who are enthusiastic had lower resting heart rates and blood pressure. They frequently feel more content, happier, and healthier. Fortunately, excitement spreads quickly and tends to influence others.

So how do we increase our intake of this elixir known as enthusiasm? To help you dig deep and find more excitement for yourself, here is an Enthusiastic Six List.

1. Become completely and intimately familiar with your products and services.

Knowing your products well and thoroughly will enable you to manage any situation that a client or prospect may present. It implies that you have a thorough understanding of how it operates, as well as its features, advantages, and how what you offer is marketed in brochures and online. It implies that you pay attention to your customers in order to comprehend how your goods and services might help them. Knowing your products and services well offers you the assurance that you are genuinely passionate and enthusiastic about what you sell.

2. Know your business.

Know its origins, tenets, and principles. comprehend the mission, and live it. Understand what it means to be a world-class player in your business and how your value offer benefits customers. Learn about your top customers, how they benefit from your goods and services, and why they continue to use you. As you gain knowledge, you'll find a new respect for the business, which will come over as excitement for your work. You will turn into a walking advertisement for why potential customers should hire you.

3. Distribute electricity.

Every commodity or service you offer has had a significant impact on your customers' businesses or even their personal lives. You must be able to convey these tales in an engaging manner. List the top five customer successes for your organization in a minute. Each tale should emphasize how your product or service helped the client achieve his or her professional or personal objectives. Practice repeating the stories again and over once you've captured them on paper. Tell your employer, your boss's boss, your prospects, and your clients about them. Also, tell your coworkers at work. Potential and present customers are curious about how your business has impacted other businesses since success generates success.

4. Individual inspiration.

People who are successful develop an image in their minds of what success looks like. They then translate that vision into precise objectives that direct their day-to-day operations. Aspirations spark excitement. Think about how happy a kid would be on Monday morning if he knew he was going to Disneyland the previous weekend.

Successful salespeople encounter the same ruts and rejections in their everyday work as the rest of us. The world of sales is not for the timid. You must be able to deal with rejection on a frequent basis if you want to achieve. Rejection is unpleasant and may stifle zeal. Personal pep speeches are crucial for this reason.

We have an inner conversation 80% of the time, according to psychologists, and talking to ourselves positively may have a significant beneficial influence on our mood, vitality, and self-confidence. Lean on your own achievement vision during pep talks to inspire the zeal you need to achieve your goals. People that are successful often compliment themselves throughout the day. Encourage yourself to overcome obstacles and strive for greatness.

5. Don't be afraid to put on a show.

Feeling and action are linked. Have you ever been so exhausted in the middle of the day that you decided to go for a walk? Usually, working out gives you new life and energy. Doctors advise exercising for those who are depressed because of this. Getting up and moving is a terrific approach to getting over lethargy or a poor attitude. It often happens that when you act ecstatic or joyful, real sensations follow.

Think it and you'll be it is a corollary to "fake it 'til you make it." According to cognitive psychologists, altering the way we think about what we're doing is the greatest way to modify how we feel about what we're doing. The body responds to the brain's instructions on how to feel. It's true that by altering our ideas, we may control our own emotions and view on life. Change your cognitive process the next time you're depressed and see what occurs. Consider the advantages of your circumstance. Consider achieving your objectives and see the results. By adopting a more optimistic thought pattern, you actually have the ability to alter how you are and the results of the future.

6. Take up exercise.

It's far simpler to muster excitement when you're in good health and have plenty of energy. There is truly no replacement for consistent exercise, a healthy diet, and adequate sleep since your body is a temple. We're not discussing finishing a marathon... A 20-minute stroll will be plenty. Your mood often follows your physical well-being.

People are drawn to individuals who exude excitement, as well as those who bring with them special chances and priceless resources. Use one of the Enthusiastic Six from the list above to try to become more enthusiastic today, and observe the results. Most likely, this will make you feel better about yourself, and your increased excitement will result.

Body Language

Humans are naturally sociable creatures, thus to fit into the wider social structure, they must blend in with the crowd. Everywhere the rule is applicable, including in business. Entrepreneurs may be the backbone of their companies, but for those companies to expand, they need staff, reliable partners, and expanding customer bases. Getting the proper individuals on board may be mostly solved by knowing body language metaphorically.

Hiring

When hiring team members, whether they are interns, senior executives, or service providers, entrepreneurs should look for people that are trustworthy, dependable, and diligent. However, an HR representative or an executive will seldom ever learn about these characteristics during the initial consultation or interview. But let's simplify things a little by using body language.

A 4-second rule is something that exists. A direct query is more likely to elicit an honest response. Do you consider yourself to be a hard worker? is a question you may ask your candidate. And after grimacing, the candidate replies, "Yes, without a doubt." It's your responsibility to interpret that face. You can tell who someone really is, or at least get quite near, if you can read their face well and compare it to the other expressions they used during the interview. The majority of applicants are prepared in terms of their posture when they are seated or have prepared their responses in a pattern, but you must constantly be one level ahead. Use the "4-second rule" to determine the solution for yourself.

Getting in Touch with Your Coworkers

It is crucial to get along well with your team now that you have one. Whether you adhere to an "Open door policy" or not is up to you. In this situation, it is crucial to distinguish between how much is too much.

If you're talking, it shouldn't be idle chitchat, and if you're making jokes, you shouldn't be laughing nonstop. According to research, warmth and compassion are necessary for receiving appreciation, but you have to recognize that adoration cannot be given to you instantly; it must be earned. You may use this simple 5-step strategy to connect with your coworkers effectively and long-term.

Look
Smile (not much, however) (not much though)

Greet (A person who is senior and welcomes a junior is regarded as more friendly) (A person who is senior and greets a junior is considered warmer)
express gratitude or praise

Seek their feedback (It could be a casual or work-related question too, just to keep the conversation intact)

Choosing Excellent Partners

We're all on the lookout for a prospective spouse. We don't want someone who is handling much less or substantially more business than we are. How can we recognize that?using their non-verbal cues. Usually, one can see the hands communicating when a person is confident. The exact reverse occurs when someone is attempting to manipulate or tell a lie, which is referred to in body language parlance as a pacifier. Using a pacifier is a self-soothing action, similar to touching oneself when stressed or anxious.

It might be difficult to tell who is truly interested in your company during a networking event. Therefore, how can you tell if someone is truly interested in your company or not? There are two easy techniques:

Leadership
It's crucial for an entrepreneur to demonstrate their leadership abilities. Being emotionally savvy falls under the category of leadership and is crucial. It simply implies that you should be aware of when what, and how to talk. Even while it seems straightforward, making the right decision may be difficult, particularly if someone on your team makes a mistake. Make sure the error is not repeated, but also that the perpetrator is aware of the error.

Successful leaders frequently display certain nonverbal cues, some of which include:

They appear convincing because they feel they can, according to their assertive body language. Before presenting a concept to clients or a team, it is crucial to be certain that it will work.
Using the open palm symbol
How do you make use of the area to your advantage (personal, social, and public)
employing pauses and a low-pitched voice with a nice pace

Lie Spotting

Every entrepreneur has what is referred to as a gut instinct, sixth sense, or intuition. This is nothing more than your brain picking up non-verbal cues from numerous situations and alerting you to a problem. But don't believe stories that claim that lying is indicated by nose rubbing, eye blocking, or hands on the face. When it comes to lying, every one of us uses a particular body language.

Although there are many ways to tell if someone is lying by their body language, baseline analysis is the most crucial and successful one. It mainly involves recognizing and noting a person's speech and body language, such as their use of their hands while speaking, facial emotions, seating positions, blink rate, breathing rate, choice of words, and manner of laughing or smiling.

Chapter 2

The Secret Of Good Salesmanship And Leadership In Business

For many business owners, closing their first transaction is a huge challenge. Numerous queries arise, such as:

- How can I differentiate my product from that of my rivals?
- What kinds of inquiries ought I to pose?
- How do I respond to criticism?
- How should I make my order request?

The following are first-time entrepreneurs' sales secrets:
1. Sell advantages rather than features. The largest error business owners make is concentrating on their product or service. Jamie argues that what matters is what it does. "An item labeled "health food" has nutrients that are excellent for the body. It is exactly that. The solution helps the user become leaner, more active, and more productive with less sleep "He clarifies. Always think about how your consumer will benefit from your goods.

2. Market to those most inclined to make a purchase. Your finest prospects are those that are very interested in your good or service and have the money to buy it. They will purchase the fastest. Jamie Louis advises against trying to sell photocopy machines to folks who

have never purchased one. "Sell to those who already own one or to people you know who would like to purchase one. Display to them how amazing yours is."

3. Make your product stand out.
Why should a consumer choose to do business with you rather than your rival? Jamie advises creating at least three elements that will persuade a buyer to make a purchase from you. "People dislike trying new things because it takes them out of their comfort zone. Give them three solid justifications for trying your goods, "Tracy elucidates. "Your product or service, for instance, performs more quickly, costs less money, and has higher-quality ingredients."

4. Make eye contact.
One of the least productive strategies for beginning business owners is to spend a lot of money on print media advertising or direct mail. The personal approach cannot be rushed. Get to know your customer—if not in person, then at least over the phone.

5. Pay attention to the second sale.
Word of mouth is responsible for producing around 85% of all sales. They come about as a result of someone recommending a good or service to a friend or acquaintance because the consumer was happy, claims Tracy. Focus instead on generating new clientele and word-of-mouth recommendations from each consumer. "The second sale must be the focus of all you do. Will

my consumer have such a positive experience that he returns to me or recommends me to his friends?"

6. Create a rapport.
Befriend your prospect before bringing up business. Do some research to establish a rapport. Check to see whether you work with someone in common. Has the prospect's business recently made headlines? Does he enjoy playing sports? Get a little background information on the organization and the person, advises Richardson, to help you establish a sincere rapport.

7. Look further.
Will you instantly explain to a prospect how your product satisfies his desire for cost-savings and efficiency if he says, "We're looking for cost-savings and efficiency"? According to Jamie, a very clever salesperson won't; instead, they'll delve deeper and ask additional questions: "I can see why it's significant. Please provide a particular example." "Ask for more information so you can properly position your product and demonstrate that you understand the client's wants," advises Richardson.

8. Develop your ear.
Salespeople who dominate a presentation by chatting nonstop usually lose the transaction in addition to boring the prospect. You should be listening at least 50% of the time. By taking notes, monitoring your prospect's body language, refraining from drawing inferences, and focusing on what your prospect is saying, you may enhance your listening abilities.

9. Know the industry of your customers. Customers anticipate that you will be as knowledgeable about their company, clients, and rivals as you are about your own goods or services. Research the industry of your customers. Be aware of its issues and tendencies. Find out who his main rivals are. The company's annual report, trade journals, chamber of commerce directories, and the company's own brochures, bulletins, and catalogs are a few examples of research resources.

10. Prepare an organized sales presentation.
Building rapport with your prospect, introducing the business issue, getting a deeper understanding of their needs through questioning, summarizing your major selling points, and closing the deal make up the fundamental format of every sales presentation. Always start the process by imagining a successful conclusion.

11. Make a list.
Don't rely on memory to help you remember what matters to your prospect. If you want to take notes during your sales presentation, make sure you get permission in advance. Make a list of important topics so you may refer to them during your presentation.

12. Request commentary.
Asking your clients what you need to do to keep and grow their company can help you improve your sales presentation and relationships with them. "Many clients have small grievances but never voice them. They just

won't purchase from you again "said Jamie. If you seek their viewpoint, they'll be happy to share it with you and provide you with the opportunity to find a solution.

(I) Time Management And Expenditure

Managers and business owners should set a good example. The decisions made by an organization's decision-makers directly affect the corporate culture and, frequently, the profitability of the firm. Business owners should always endeavor to enhance or improve their personal time management skills since it increases a company's efficiency and effectiveness.

One of the most crucial talents to possess is time management, yet both organizations and individuals frequently struggle with the idea. Particularly small firms cannot afford to lose time via ineffective time management. The advantages of effective time management techniques, however, are enormous. Businesses that manage their time well are more likely to regularly provide their goods or services on schedule.

A company with effective time management is also able to address issues as they emerge without having a material negative effect on regular business operations. A planned, organized timetable gives extra time for problem-solving or unanticipated occurrences, which is crucial for firms that depend on steady output to boost ROI.

Owners of businesses can and ought to foster a culture where time management is valued. The following advice is provided to business owners to help them better manage time at work.

Prioritize
Setting each task's priority will assist you in maintaining concentration and achieving both your daily and long-term objectives. Think about what must be completed before the day is through. Prioritize each item according to its urgency, such as a deadline, and work your way down the list. You may rest easier knowing that the most time-sensitive chores have already been attended to if something unforeseen occurs throughout the day.

Set Measurable Objectives
Both business owners and workers need to know this. You may evaluate the effectiveness of your effort and keep track of your progress toward a goal by setting specific objectives. You should inquire about things as a business like "Where do we want to be at this point next year? How much money must we bring in the following month to stay on schedule?"

The responses to your inquiries should result in specific, quantifiable objectives that you can share with your staff. Time management entails being productive with your time while also directing that productivity toward attaining the objectives of your business.

Think ahead
You will have less time and unneeded worry tomorrow if you plan ahead today. Once your objectives are clear, you can start creating a realistic schedule for achieving them.

Being realistic about what you can do and how soon you can complete the timetable is a crucial component of planning. Avoid the pitfall of being excessively ambitious with each deadline. Although time is money, it is always more important to give yourself adequate time to create a high-quality good or service. Setting unattainable objectives and failing to explain to your team what needs to be done to fulfill them will only serve to demoralize your team members.

Recognize when to assign
Your time as a business owner is frequently split between ongoing tasks and more significant obligations. You can save a lot of time if you know when it's okay to assign some of those responsibilities to other team members. It's a fantastic chance to inspire your staff by giving them new challenges and responsibilities.

Calculating how long it would take someone else to finish the work is an excellent technique to decide what can and cannot be outsourced. Would it require more training? Would evaluating their work take longer than it would for me to do it myself? You should consider all of these issues before deciding whether to delegate.

Planning your week is the key to good time management – whether you're a one-person business working from home or a growing start-up. Creating a schedule for your week allows you to plan ahead and structure your time so that you can prioritize and re-prioritize tasks – all while cutting down on your stress levels, to boot.

Small business time management can be tricky, so start with the essentials. Deadlines and urgent jobs should define how you organize tasks across your week. For example, if you've got a big deliverable on Thursday, make the days leading up to production days, and leave non-urgent but important tasks like admin and meetings for Friday.

Be ready to reorganize your schedule if priorities suddenly change, too. Think of it as a 'Plan A' or a work in progress rather than something set in stone.

Group tasks by project or type one of the most effective time management strategies when it comes to planning your week is group tasks. It can be helpful to arrange similar or related activities together on a single day, so that you're not hopping from one thing to another, and can focus on the specific goals you need to achieve. For example, you might dedicate a whole day to working on marketing tasks like social media and writing your newsletter, as the tasks will relate to each other and you can apply your creative flow to several things at once. Keep in mind this time management approach works for methodical jobs too. You might spend an afternoon doing invoices, which will be quicker in a batch because the same steps are repeated and you'll get faster as you go along.

Create a day-by-day schedule

A proper structure is the backbone of a planned week, and there are lots of ready-made templates available online that you can download and fill in to itemize your days. These can work for individuals or whole teams. A good template should give equal weight to each day, and have enough space to write a few words about each task or target – not too much though, or it just becomes cluttered.

If you're a one-person business and you like to plan on paper, you could start getting organized with a Notebook to keep track of your week and make sure your schedule is always at hand.

Plan for distraction

It's not realistic to plan productivity and focus for every hour of every day, so don't set your business' time management strategy up to fail. The best time management systems are all about balance! Instead, expect to be distracted, disrupted, and confronted by unexpected challenges and opportunities. When you're planning for the week ahead, add 'interruption time' – a proportion of the day when you don't expect to spend every moment getting work done.

So although your office hours might be 9 til 5 with an hour for lunch, you can realistically deduct an hour from the total. Don't think of that as wasted time, however –

what feels like a frustrating delay will help you refresh your mind and might even be the moment inspiration strikes.

Dive into deep work
The idea of deep work is that you're consciously focusing on your task and training your attention away from distractions. To achieve that, you need to be able to carve out time when you'll be free of meetings and other commitments, and able to focus fully on one task. Put time for deep work into your weekly schedule, and support your intentions by blocking this time off from distractions and interruptions. A 'do not disturb sign and an email auto-reply is a good start to apply this time management strategy.

Organize your day's work
What does a typical workday look like for small business owners? A common answer is that there is no typical day – various and exciting activities are a hallmark of life as an entrepreneur. That doesn't mean you can't organize your time, however. A daily plan is valuable even if it changes, as it can help you keep track of priorities, deadlines, and your progress on longer-term goals. As with your weekly approach, the trick is to have a fluid schedule that can flex and adapt to new things, rather than a rigid timetable.
Here are a few more time management tips to help you plan how to spend your day.

Keep priorities in check with a to-do list

A business time management classic, the to-do is a list of the things you want or need to get done within your day, organized according to priority. The most urgent and important things should be at the top and less important or postponable things towards the bottom. But keep in mind, a long to-do list will just cause you unnecessary stress.

Target your efforts with time-blocking
Time blocking is a time management technique that many small business owners find useful. It's the practice of chunking out your work into dedicated sections of time – the opposite of multitasking, where attention is spread inefficiently across multiple activities at once. The idea is that by focusing on one thing at a time, you can dedicate attention and energy to each task and get it done more quickly and to a higher standard. This a great way to approach work if you're wondering how to manage time as a business owner.
To time-block your day, you need to schedule the hours you have available and assign them to items on your to-do list. For effective time management, you won't necessarily do the most important thing on the list first thing in the morning. Instead, you should assign your top task to the part of the day when you know you'll be most productive. If you're a morning person, that could be the first thing. If you're a night owl, the late afternoon might be when you really hit your stride.
If you tend to feel sleepy after lunch – most of us do –, spend that time doing necessary but low-effort things like paperwork or timesheets.

The key to being productive is having good time management skills. Your total productivity may be greatly affected by how you prioritize and determine how much time should be dedicated to each work. It's a talent that should be developed at both the employee and management levels to increase the effectiveness of your company.

A key component of effective time management is making sure that the time spent on each work is directly correlated with its significance to the company. This implies that both personnel and management spend the bulk of their time on the most useful duties and the least amount of time on activities that are not as important. This is obviously easier said than done. Work out the following first in order to do this:

- Which tasks should be prioritized?
- What duties are less crucial?
- What chores can be postponed, handed off, or ignored?
- Which critical activities need the completion of less critical (possibly "important") tasks first?

Only after that can you choose which duties should be dealt with in what sequence and priorlty.

Staff time management that works

By prioritizing their tasks in this way, you may assist your workers in time management. If employees are overburdened with several little tasks that take up too much of their time, productivity may suffer. Planning their schedule around their primary objectives is the key to resolving this.

Every employee on your team should be aware of:
- Their key objectives (and tasks needed to achieve them)
- The supplemental activities needed to accomplish their primary objectives
- How do their objectives and duties compare to those of their coworkers
- The obstacles that can cause them to be late or fail to complete their major objectives
- How much of each day should be devoted to their primary and supporting duties

Assist each employee in developing a time management plan that specifies the amount of time each kind of work should take based on the information provided. If it still appears like auxiliary duties are taking up too much time, you may need to take additional action, such as assigning those jobs to more employees or determining which tasks may be reduced or eliminated entirely.

Other time management advice is as follows:
making daily to-do lists in accordance with the time management strategy
Developing the ability to say "No!" to more work when it conflicts with current priorities
limiting distractions like email, phones, and social media by setting specific times of day for checking and using them (blanket bans tend to be counterproductive)

Reduce the frequency of meetings and make sure those that do occur are scheduled to last as little time as possible.

As organizations struggle to stay up with technology advancements or when employee turnover results in certain less-than-ideal methods of doing jobs being passed on to new hires, inefficiencies can occasionally develop over time. You should routinely (e.g. once a year) carry out "efficiency audits" of your processes to ensure that everything is still going as smoothly as possible.

managing their time as business owners

Your approach to time management has to be somewhat different since you are the company's owner and director. You must have a comprehensive understanding of what is happening throughout your whole organization, but there may also be crucial responsibilities that you alone are capable of doing. Decide what is the best use of your time (as opposed to someone else's time) by taking extra care.

Here are a few pieces of advice:

Delegate

As a general guideline, only do a task if no one else inside the organization is able to. As much as possible, keep your job to "boss work." Here, an accountant may be a big assistance.

Schedule

Plan your day carefully, and don't let meetings go past their allotted time. Set aside long periods of time to complete tasks as well; it's difficult to concentrate if your breaks are only 30 minutes long.

Rationalize
Make sure everything you do has a clear connection to at least one of your company objectives. If a link isn't visible right away, consider if you really need to do this action.

Time management techniques for boosting productivity
By minimizing the amount of time lost each day, effective time management may significantly boost productivity.

Other important advantages are:
- Teams may communicate more efficiently, resulting in fewer "blocks" and less downtime.
- Important tasks are given the necessary time and are not hurried.
- You complete tasks on time without rushing to the finish.
- You lessen the need for overtime labor and late shifts, which makes your team happy.

By figuring out who could have some extra time, you can handle small ad hoc work and disturbances.

You can rapidly determine and manage workload concerns, for example, by determining whether a job is running late.

Expenditure

It might be challenging to determine what is considered an expense in the beginning, especially if you operate as a lone proprietor. Do you even know what kind of expense it is if you are aware that it is a company expense?

Have no concerns if you are unsure about your capital costs. But we're here to correct you. Here is our overview of company expenses and how to keep track of them.

What exactly is a business expense?
In its widest sense, a business expense is a cash you spend "wholly and entirely" on that enterprise. Applying this concept is straightforward when you pay expenses that are only for your company, such as office supplies. Just when a cost is only partially related to your company activity does it become challenging.

Once your company is up and running, it is crucial to carefully plan and oversee its financial performance. The most efficient strategy to keep your company's finances on track is to establish a budgeting procedure.

This manual teaches how to do it and describes the benefits of company planning and budgeting. It offers suggestions for actions that may be taken to improve the financial management of your company and guarantee the viability of your ambitions.

Creating a plan for commercial success

It's simple to become mired in day-to-day issues while managing a business and lose sight of the greater picture. Successful firms, on the other hand, take the time to design and revise business strategies, generate and manage budgets, and keep a close eye on their finances and performance.

Planning in a structured manner may greatly influence your company's expansion. You will be able to focus your efforts on boosting revenue, cutting expenses, and boosting returns on investment.

In reality, even without a formal process, many organizations perform the bulk of business planning-related tasks, including considering potential development regions, rivals, cash flow, and profit.

It doesn't have to be challenging or time-consuming to turn this into a coherent procedure to manage the growth of your firm. The most crucial factor is that plans be created, are dynamic, and shared with all parties involved. To learn what to put in your yearly plan, refer to the page in this handbook.

The main advantage of business planning is that it enables you to define your company's direction and sets goals that will promote expansion. Additionally, it will provide you the chance to take a step back and assess your performance and the variables impacting your company. Planning your business can provide:

- a stronger capacity to continuously improve and foresee issues
- dependable financial data for decision-making
- increased confidence in your decision-making, clarity, and concentration

What information should be in your yearly plan

Your yearly business plan's primary goal is to lay out your company's strategy and action plan. Included in this should be a clear financial picture of where you are now and where you hope to go in the upcoming year. Your yearly business plan should contain the following:

A list of the modifications you intend to make to your company possible alterations to your market, consumers, and competitors

your yearly goals and objectives, as well as your key performance indicators

any concerns or issues

operational alterations

details about your management, personnel, financial performance, and projections

specifics of the business investment

Planning for a business is most successful when it is a continuous process. As a result, you may take swift action when it's essential rather than just responding to things as they happen.

A typical cycle for company planning

Compare your present performance to your goals from the previous or current year.

- Prepare a list of your opportunities and dangers.

- Examine your achievements and setbacks from the preceding year.
- Examine your main goals for the upcoming year, then adjust or reestablish your long-term strategy.
- Create a budget and identify and improve the resource implications of your evaluation.
- Set goals for the balance sheet and profit and loss for the upcoming fiscal year.
- Finish the plan. By keeping an eye on performance, assessing progress, and meeting goals, evaluate it frequently—for instance, once a month.

Finances and strategic planning

New small business owners could operate their companies casually and not recognize the necessity for budgeting. However, if you are making plans for your company, you will need money to support those ambitions. The best method to manage your cash flow and invest in fresh prospects at the right moment is through budgeting.

You might not always be able to manage every aspect of your developing company. You might need to allocate different portions of your budget to things like sales, production, and marketing. You'll notice that money starts to flow through your organization in a variety of different routes. Budgets are an essential tool for

ensuring that you maintain control over spending. Creating a budget involves:
- Take charge of your finances
- Be sure you can afford your present obligations, so you can make informed financial decisions and achieve your goals.
- Make sure you have sufficient funds for your next initiatives.

It describes what you'll buy with your money and how you'll pay for it. It is not a forecast, though. A budget is a planned outcome of the future that your organization is aiming to attain, as opposed to a projection, which is a prediction of the future. Costs are important, very important. Most business owners are aware of this in the early stages and stress over every dollar spent.

However, as the company expands, they discover that it can no longer keep a careful eye on every dollar spent. Here are ideas to assist your business manage expenditures as you grow.

Consolidate your purchases so you may bargain for lower prices. By consolidating their print and mailing house services into one company, one executive we work with was able to save her company over $100,000 annually on their $1 million annual direct mail budget. Also, keep in mind that reviewing your key vendors is crucial for businesses that have recently experienced a growth spurt. We frequently observe businesses paying prices based on significantly higher purchasing quantities. Negotiate again often. This one piece of advice has helped our business coaching clients save millions of dollars.

Additionally, look around your neighborhood for local buying groups that bring together all the neighborhood companies and use their combined purchasing power on behalf of all the members.

Encourage suppliers to compete for your patronage.
It's astonishing how much better your price can be when your vendors feel the hot breath of their competitors on their necks. Make sure they are aware of each other without shoving it in their faces.

Even if you want to stick with your present supplier, the knowledge that you and they are seeking outside quotes will encourage them to maintain their prices competitive and increase the likelihood that you will receive better terms.

Regularly review your vendors.
Building on the previous suggestion, have your firm establish an annual or semi-annual evaluation of all of its important vendors. You should also be sure to highlight all automatically renewing contracts so that they appear for review and rebidding sixty to ninety days before their renewal.

Better still, strike out the boilerplate clause that mandates an automatic renewal in your vendor's contract and replace it with wording that states you have the option but not the duty to renew.

Teach your team how to request and receive discounts.

Increased cash flow results generously from quick negotiating training on how your team may obtain reductions from your vendors, as well as a regular appreciation of team members that achieve this.

(II) The Secret Of Winning Clients And Accumulation Of Market Power

One fundamental truth never changes: For a firm to succeed, there must be clients.

1. Take your clients where they are.

We group our locations together in areas where our clients live, work, and play because we want to be their neighborhood beauty shop. Instead of attempting to alter our consumers' behavior, we integrate into their lifestyle by going to where they exercise, have coffee, and conduct errands.

For us, this tactic is a strong acquisition model. When a consumer comes in hot from yoga and feels at ease grabbing mascara or asking for cosmetic tips, we know we've done something well.

2. Keep in touch constantly.

How long do you want to run your business? Act accordingly whether the response is 10, 20, or 30 years. Too many businesspeople work month to month. Their actions are all momentary, and they never develop a long-lasting business model. They generally lose as a result.

Keep in touch with consumers by calling, texting, emailing, or using social media. Referrals come from consistently demonstrating your worth. People often transact business with people they know rather than those to whom they are only introduced. You are more likely to attract and retain clients the more attention you receive.

3. Become animated.

People also purchase from you when you sell something to them. Your closing rate is closely correlated with how you market yourself. Consider this: You hear two firms present identical pitches. However, you can tell when a person is more active that they genuinely want to win your company. Whom would you pick?

You can't pretend to be excited. You must sincerely care about your clients' requirements and want to fulfill their demands. Go above and above to make sure they continue to experience your enthusiasm for serving them after they become a customer. Don't make them wait for the outcome. Give them a "fast victory" that exceeds their expectations so they will have greater faith in your abilities and enthusiasm for working with you.

4. Recognize their problems, and gain their trust.

It's important to comprehend your customers' problems. Query your audience to learn their needs. It may imply the difference between launching a sale that everyone should make and a failure. Use your client's own words to guide everything from sales emails to social media posts and ad text after conducting a survey to learn about their problems.

Then, as the last surprise, give them something more to make sure they're content, like a handwritten message, a call, or a present. Build a small following of devoted clients who know, like, and trust you and will sing your praises to their friends since it is simpler to sell to an existing customer than to get a new one.

5. Discuss with them.

Create engaging, trustworthy, and problem-solving content. Customers desire the ability to interact with your brand and actual people. Videos and webinars are excellent for in-person connection that fosters rapport. Live video, which can include presentations and product demos, offers a more individualized, hands-on purchasing experience.

Educate your audience and offer clear, tangible advantages. Give them a concrete answer to their problem and concentrate on it.

6. Take in what they are saying.

Simply said, listen and participate. Customers will communicate their needs and preferences to you. Use social media to interact with them, or send out surveys in your emails. Make sure your website is simple to use on both desktop and mobile devices, and that people can contact you easily if they run into trouble.

Deal with issues swiftly, formally, and regrettably to make your consumer feel valued and let them know how much you value their company. They are more likely to return if you offer them what they want and keep the channels of communication open.

7. Offer them what they desire.

In the end, attracting customers boils down to two considerations:

- Do you fulfill their needs or desires
- Can they locate you?

Describe how your product or service benefits clients, then concentrate on interaction. Discover the private, sensitive information about their motivations for engaging with your company. After that, build a lifetime of memorable interactions with your brand. Because of this, your consumer scrolls through your rivals without pausing. Add value that has an impact.

8. Be sincere.

The foundation of enduring partnerships is trust. Inform your clients of the action you're intending to take, then accomplish it and let them know. then carry on.

Become essential and add value at all times. Be a step ahead of your consumers and anticipate their needs. Maintain high standards and go above and beyond. Own your faults and seek corrections; don't provide justifications. Never let up on your efforts since you are only as good as your previous one.

9. Provide the greatest product you can.

You must provide a superior product or service since consumers now have more options than before. Either create money for your customers or save them money and time. Examine your competitors. Offer a premium product that customers will pay extra for rather than competing on pricing. It's crucial to have a stellar reputation and reviews because most people conduct internet research before making a purchase.

Excellent marketing attracts new clients. Address an issue, present a fix, and set your good or service apart. Keep your customers happy by keeping your commitments. To enhance your offering, collect feedback and innovate.

(III) The Strategy Of Closing A Sales

Theoretically, understanding how to close a deal is rather straightforward: arrive prepared, deliver your presentation, address any concerns raised by your prospect, ask for the sale, and, if necessary, follow up until you receive a clear response.

I've spent numerous hours closing (and attempting to close) deals during my career, but in reality, selling is a little more difficult than that. Avoiding sales closing sins is difficult, especially if you're new to the industry.

The process of closing a transaction is as much an art form as it is a scientific one, even though there is an underlying formula. The finest closing questions to get your prospect to say yes will be discussed along with some of the most effective sales closing approaches.

Let's start with some of the fundamental science behind why sales don't close, and where you could be wasting your efforts if you're ready.

Be a master of negotiation.

Learn a straightforward strategy for closing more lucrative agreements. Of course, one of the greatest ways to increase the number of potential clients who sign on the dotted line is by learning new sales strategies to add to your toolkit and evaluating which ones perform best in your sales process.

These are the top 12 sales closing strategies that will enable you to assess any circumstance and replace those resounding "no" responses with your persuasive arguments.

The Presumed Close

The Assumptive Close is predicated on the idea that you have confidence in your ability to close this deal from the minute you start working on it. The key is checking on your prospect regularly, measuring their degree of interest, resolving obstacles, and figuring out if they're on the same page as you.

Why it works:

Your optimism and self-assurance make the prospect believe that the solution should be as simple to them as it is to you.

When it works best:

When you're dealing with known leads and are confident that your offering is the ideal solution for their needs.

When not to utilize it:

If you don't already have a rapport with your prospect and you keep getting feedback that the solution isn't practical for them.

The Close Now or Never

Provide an incentive to your potential customer that they can only receive if they commit within a specified time frame (including today). This may consist of:

The only [product] we have left is this. 15% off is offered to everyone who signs up right now. If you join right away, you can go ahead in the line for implementation. This offer is only valid until [date], so act quickly.

Why it works:

Since the potential customer now feels as though they are missing out on something, it only makes sense to ask for their business now rather than later.

When it works best:

When you are free to provide discounts and you are interacting with individuals whose major argument is that they don't have enough time to make a decision right now.

When not to utilize it:

When the potential customer has said that your product will never be implemented at their firm or when you are unable to provide a sizable incentive.

Close The Takeaway

This idea is straightforward: remove some components from the discussion if you've previously given out the benefits for them and they don't appear interested in them. Offer to cut costs by deleting product features they might not require, and then observe whether they are more likely to accept the offer.

Why it works:

The price alone causes many people to protest. Everyone will benefit if you can overcome that obstacle by taking away stuff they don't need.

Some Powerful Sales Techniques for Quicker Deal Closing

Explosive growth might result from cutting the sales cycle short. Here are a few tried-and-true tactics for closing agreements more quickly.

The way consumers make judgments about their purchases is continuously evolving, so it's critical to regularly review your sales approach with your personnel. It may be difficult to strike the right balance between being convincing and without being conceited or obnoxious while selling any kind of good or service.

This requires careful preparation, but thankfully you can ensure that your business is consistent and closing more transactions with a strong strategy in place. Keep in mind that the consumer should always come first while trying to close a deal. The best methods to help you close sales more quickly are listed below:

Determine who made the choice.
The key to a rapid closing is understanding the decision maker, regardless of the business you are in. In order to learn as much as they can about your business, the decision-makers frequently throw someone else into the fray. If this is the case, be sure to imagine yourself as the decision-shoe maker so that you can tailor your sales pitch to suit their preferences, even if they aren't there.
Of course, meeting the decision-maker face-to-face is the ideal situation. Make every effort to arrange a meeting with that person.

Be truthful
During the sales process, a client can tell if you are being sincere or not. In other words, it's critical to demonstrate to the client that you value their company beyond the transaction. Being too methodical might turn people off, but keep in mind that being organized is also acceptable. Just don't behave as if you don't care about the client's best interests; it's OK to seem prepared for any questions that come your way.

Establish a feeling of urgency

To encourage the customer to commit, provide a deadline in the agreement. Make them feel in control by offering a discount or something for free. This does not entail pressuring the consumer; rather, it simply implies that you should make an extra effort to convince them that your good or service is the best option—and the best option right now.

Defeat opposition
Any contract may go more quickly if the sales presentation is prepared to anticipate and overcome any objections. It can be necessary to spend some time coming up with a solution if anything catches you off guard. Sales guru Tom Searcy referred to this as having a "landmine map" in a previous Inc. piece.
You may lessen resistance by establishing a list of potential issues and a careful examination of the dangers.
I strongly advise going down with your complete sales team and asking each member to brainstorm potential objections. See if there are any obstacles you and your team could have missed as you present your sales proposal to them.

Understand your competition
It's hard to compete for business. Knowing the areas where you excel more than your rivals will help you clinch the deal quickly. Again, preparedness is the key here. Do your homework and be careful to highlight everything you are doing that is different from what your

rivals are doing. Considering that this is frequently the main selling factor, you shouldn't overlook it.

Watch your language

Don't stutter when speaking. Focus on your areas of expertise and keep it brief. Although you must maintain your professionalism, you want to be genuine and approachable.

(IV) Learning From Competitors And Boost Sales

To expand your business, study your rivals. Most small businesses have an unpleasant feature, which is the mindset of being wary of or viewing their rivals as their enemy. Even if they are vying for the same clients as you are, they may still benefit you far more than harm you.

The first fundamental rule of competing firms is that if several companies are providing the same good or service in a similar geographic region, then there is a sizable enough market to support them all. A form of natural selection kicks in if it turns out that there isn't a big enough demand for that product.

If there aren't enough customers to support the less successful businesses on the lower end, those businesses will inevitably go out of business unless they pivot in some way or find a way to scale up. This is how the market corrects itself: the limited number of customers who are interested in a particular product will gravitate towards the businesses that are the best.

This indicates that if you're still operating and doing well, you and your competitors are among the companies that your market favors. If that is the case, you don't really need to be concerned about a rival driving you out of business since you can really grow your own company by studying those rival companies.

Look into the Competition

Finding out who your competitors are is the first step you should take if you want to learn from them. Finding out for sure is the first step to utilizing their knowledge. Depending on the industry you operate in, you may not have many rivals at all.

If you've been involved in your community, you may have met some of your competitors already, which isn't always a bad thing. By keeping in contact with the local business community, you can learn what your rivals are up to and whether or not anything they're doing is applicable to your own company.

A face-to-face conversation with other business owners in your industry is a lot more effective approach to getting to know them and discovering how they manage their operations than just searching the internet for as much information as you can.

Look up competing businesses in online directories.

But that functions as well. When it's possible, you should also arrange a meet-and-greet with a fellow business owner in addition to using the internet to research your rivals as much as you can. Several methods exist for locating your rivals.

Searching via multiple channels for other companies that offer the same goods or services as you do is a fantastic place to start. The easiest route is to check listings on websites like Yelp, YP (the website for the Yellow Pages), local directories in your community like the Chamber of Commerce, and any other sites you can discover with business listings arranged by category.

When you locate firms that are comparable to your own, you may further investigate them to see whether their goods or services are the same as yours and to determine whether or not they are your direct rivals.

Learn from Their Mistakes

These can be some of the most valuable lessons to take from competitors. There's no reason that you should repeat the same mistakes which other businesses in your field have already made, just because you were unaware of those mistakes. The only challenge with this method is finding out what those mistakes are.

To begin, you may even be able to simply ask a competitor, directly, what problems they've had and what kinds of things have not worked out for them. Taking this direct approach won't always work, and you might have trouble just getting in touch with the owner of a business.

Many business owners, however, will be happy to give you a bit of advice on what to avoid or watch out for, as a kind of professional courtesy. An experienced entrepreneur knows that you're not a threat just because you want some advice for improving how you run your business.

They know that they're already established with their own business and won't lose their existing customers or new sales because you're just not a threat to them. As we mentioned before, the size of the market in a given field is sufficient to provide customers to all the competitors in that space, simply because there are enough customers to go around (if there are enough customers to go around in that instance).

Learn What to Watch Out For

Learning about pitfalls that you can avoid before they happen can save you a lot of time and money that you would otherwise waste. Something you can do to identify those pitfalls is to look at ongoing mistakes that are happening right now in your competitors' companies.

What you do is observe a competitor's business, watch for things that they appear to be doing wrong, and make a note of it so that you can avoid those things. This is a valuable strategy because what it allows you to do is essentially pinpoint mistakes in a business like yours and completely avoid them, without ever having to suffer the consequences of those mistakes, yourself.

It's kind of like when your Grandma tells you not to mess around with that girl you're with because she knows the girl is trouble, and you actually listen to her and get rid of the girl before things get ugly. You can avoid mistakes without ever needing to go through them.

Look at Your Competitors' Customer Reviews

In the same way that you can learn valuable information from your own business reviews, you can learn from competing for business reviews, too. Most small businesses are not going to be doing this kind of research, but they should be because the what better place is there to gather information about how your competitors are actually performing, than the customers, themselves?

You can obtain all kinds of useful insights from reading your competitors' customer reviews, mostly because you're getting the information, unadulterated. And depending on how you want to process that information, you can either search their comments for specific complaints people had about the product, or you can just read through them and take the comments as they come.

Get Specific Details from Customer Comments

- What are people saying about their product?
- What did they like about it, and what did they hate?

Once you start looking through the reviews more deeply, you'll get a comprehensive picture of how people are responding to your competitor's company, which can quickly inform the strategy, structure, etc. that you should be using for your own company.

Just looking at the number of people who respond in a generally positive way, and how many responded negatively, can give you a lot of insight. One other aspect that can be really useful is to look at the reviews for a product that you're planning to release but haven't released yet.

This way, you can see how it's working out for your competitor first, to help you decide if you will need to change your thinking about that product, or if you want to offer it at all.

Customers Have a Lot to Say

You may not get the exact, specific details that you're looking for, but you'll be surprised how much information you find about a business, just from the content in those customer reviews.

When a customer writes a review for a business, they have some things to say, and they're usually going to give some details about the experience they had with that business. That's the kind of thing that you want to see when you're doing your research, the description from a customer of exactly what it was like to be a customer.

You will naturally want to see the negative reviews so that you can find out exactly what you should not be doing, but the positive reviews are helpful, too, because they will tell you when to double down on certain elements that people really liked.

Competition is a Good Thing

Your competitors are going to be there whether you like it or not, so while they are there, you might as well get something from them. What you can get from them is main knowledge, but if you just pay attention to how your competitors run their businesses, you can learn a lot more than that.

First of all, the fact that you have competitors is a really good sign because it means there's a large market for what you're selling, and customers are paying attention. Both you and the other businesses like you are all trying to do the same thing. That being the case, you can take what they have learned, what is making them successful, and where they fall short.

All you really have to do is pay attention to your competitors, and you'll be able to figure out how to reach your customers, what strategies are going to work, and which ones will not.

Chapter 3

Affiliate Marketing

In the context of advertising, affiliate marketing refers to the practice of paying outside publications to direct customers to a company's goods and services. The commission payment encourages the affiliate third-party publications to look for methods to advertise the business.

KEY LESSONS
A corporation pays partners in an affiliate marketing program for sales generated by the affiliate's promotional efforts.
Affiliate marketing has become a billion-dollar industry thanks to digital marketing, analytics, and cookies.
Affiliates are often paid per sale, and less commonly by clicks or impressions, by businesses.

Knowledge of affiliate marketing
Affiliate marketing has become more popular thanks to the internet. By developing an affiliate marketing program, which allows websites and bloggers to include links to the Amazon page for a reviewed or discussed product in exchange for advertising money when a purchase is made, Amazon (AMZN) popularized the practice. The act of selling is outsourced over a wide

network in affiliate marketing, which is effectively a pay-for-performance marketing business.

Although affiliate marketing predates the Internet, it became a billion-dollar industry in the realm of digital marketing thanks to analytics and cookies. An organization running an affiliate marketing program may monitor the links that generate leads and determine how many of them result in sales using internal analytics.

Particular Considerations
This technique aims to boost sales and provide an outcome that benefits both the merchant and the affiliate. The system is distinct, lucrative, and gaining popularity.
The model is becoming simpler to use as a result of the internet and developing technology. The way that businesses track and pay commissions on eligible leads has improved. The ability to track leads and sales more effectively helps companies develop and market their goods more effectively.

Understanding what goes into affiliate marketing as well as its benefits and drawbacks can help those who are interested in it. Businesses looking for affiliates will gain from thoroughly screening and selecting their partners. In general, it is a low-cost, efficient method of promoting goods and services, raising brand recognition, and growing a clientele.

Unattached affiliate marketing is a kind of advertising where the affiliate is not associated with the item or service being advertised. They do not represent an authority on its use or make claims about it since they lack any knowledge of associated skills or experience. This is affiliate marketing at its most basic. The affiliate is relieved of its obligation to recommend or advise due to its lack of ties to the potential consumer and product.

Related Affiliate Marketing
As its name implies, related affiliate marketing entails the promotion of goods or services by a partner who has some connection to the product or service being offered. A relationship often exists between the affiliate's specialization and the item or service. The affiliate is a credible source since they possess the authority and knowledge necessary to drive traffic. However, the affiliate provides no guarantees on the effectiveness of the commodity or service.

Affiliate marketing that is more involved creates a stronger bond between the affiliate and the item or service they are endorsing. They have used or are using the product, and they are sure that others will benefit from hearing about their great experiences. They act as reliable sources of information, and their experiences are the advertising. On the other side, given that they are making recommendations, any issues with the offering might damage their reputation.

Affiliates can be anything from a single person to a sizable corporation. The marketing is done in this area. A companion's job is to advertise one or more affiliate items in order to draw in and influence potential clients to buy the concerned product.

The Client: (Buyer)
The core of the affiliate network is the customer, often known as the consumer. The scenario is flipped since, without sales, there would be no commissions or earnings to be shared. The affiliate will use all available channels to get in touch with the customer, including social media, digital billboards, content marketing on blogs posted on search engines, and other channels of contact.

Its network (Escrow)
Only a small percentage of affiliate marketers are worried about the network. Affiliate marketing, on the other hand, serves as a vital link between affiliates and merchants and is crucial to the success of any affiliate marketing plan. If a merchant (Seller) sells their goods through a single affiliate network, companions may be required to operate through an affiliate network differently while selling a product for safety concerns.

The affiliate network also acts as a clearinghouse for a variety of affiliate programs that affiliate marketers may use to advertise their goods.

Recognize that selecting an area of interest that you are passionate about or that you are interested in might be difficult. The good news is that you can learn this information using a few techniques far more rapidly than you would think. But let's first choose a market category.

So, in this sense, what precisely is a niche?
For instance, diabetic goods may be thought of as a separate niche market. The market share of items that are connected to health is much higher than that of other categories. A smaller audience than items for general health and well-being, diabetic products target a specialized market sector. Diabetic side effects might also be advantageous for those trying to improve their health.

What are a few of your interests?
This is a simple method of identifying your target market. You should ask yourself, "What is the topic area that I am most interested in?" It's possible that this is a non-sporting event.

One well-known specialty is losing weight, to provide a few instances. You might not be able to perform as effectively as you could since you're inexperienced and fresh to the situation. Therefore, go for a less competitive option if at all feasible. Having a huge fish in a small tank is better to have a tiny fish in a large tank.

Promotional tactics include email marketing.

Having a mailing list of email subscribers will give you a big edge. As a result, it will be simple and quick for you to compose emails that contain links to affiliate offers. If people click on your affiliate links and complete their transactions on the merchant's website, the amount of money you may make from their purchases is practically endless.

Product Evaluations and Reviews
By posting product reviews, you may advertise affiliate items on your website and boost traffic. Instead of creating a biased review of a product or service in order to receive a commission, focus only on the advantages of the item or service. If you write in this way, your readers will accomplish your objectives far more rapidly. However, they won't be deterred from buying the good or service.

(I) Fundamentals And Benefits Of Social Media Marketing

Understanding the principles of digital marketing is crucial since it encompasses all contemporary marketing strategies and is a developing marketing trend.

Digital marketing is the promotion of your good or service via digital channels. It involves marketing using internet channels and is comparable to the antithesis of traditional marketing.

Understanding the principles of digital marketing is crucial since it encompasses all contemporary marketing strategies and is a developing marketing trend. For many firms, it has opened up a wide range of opportunities, and every brand must now use digital marketing strategies to successfully run their operations.

Let's first explore the importance of digital marketing for your business before delving into its principles. Here are a few justifications for why digital marketing is crucial for your company:

Cost Effective

Digital marketing initiatives demand very little upfront money. This benefits small enterprises greatly. Basic functionalities are typically offered for free by digital marketing platforms. Making the greatest use of them is up to the businesses. View this ranking of the top 10 digital marketing tools.

Greater Reach and Wider Reach

The reach of internet marketing is extensive. As a result, you are not restricted to a certain region and can accept orders for your good or service from anywhere in the globe. Additionally, you may still target a certain demographic while going global. Thus, everyone benefits.

Expanding your client

The difficulty with small enterprises is that one must develop a clientele. This is predicated on developing a rapport with a loyal consumer base. Large firms have slightly different issues. They must maintain their current client and concentrate on building their brand's reputation, customer retention, and company expansion.

Brand Recognition
Customer conversions cannot be made if they are unaware of your brand. Brand presence is crucial for addressing this. Pay-per-click advertising and other sponsored promotions can significantly increase the number of clients that visit your small business.

What is the Digital Marketing Fundamentals Elements?

SEO
"Search engine optimization" is known as SEO. It simply refers to the process of making changes to your website to make it more visible when users search for goods or services associated with your company on Google, Bing, and other search engines.

The more visible your pages are in search results, the more likely it is that you'll get noticed and draw both new and returning clients to your company. Bots are used by search engines like Google and Bing to crawl online pages by moving between websites, gathering data about them, and indexing them. The more visibility one may get through a search, the greater the likelihood of drawing attention and possible customers. It illustrates the significance of SEO.

People now prefer the Internet to other sources of information, therefore companies that want to be found and ranked in searches must invest in SEO strategies.The most natural approach to getting visitors is through SEO. The Google ranking system is rather complicated, thus the following remarks are for anyone interested in learning more about it:
Google seeks out web pages with reliable, pertinent data about user queries.They analyze the content of your website and use an algorithm to decide if it is relevant to the searcher's needs, largely based on the keywords it includes.

Numerous factors are taken into consideration when determining "quality," but one of the most important is the quantity and caliber of other websites that connect to your page and your entire site. It investigates user interaction with your website. Whether or not they click on another link after finding the information they require, return to the search results page, or stay on your website? Or do they simply not click through when they see your item in search results?

Content Promotion
Businesses that employ content marketing see growth rates that are around 30% greater than those that don't.A well-defined audience must be attracted and acquired through the use of valuable, timely, and

consistent content to motivate lucrative consumer action.

It is a long-term approach that focuses on developing a close bond with your target audience by regularly providing them with high-quality content that is pertinent to them.Customers will eventually choose you out of loyalty while making a transaction. They will buy your goods and pick them above alternatives offered by rivals. Content marketing, as opposed to one-time advertising, demonstrates your concern for your audience.
When we refer to content, we don't only mean blogs. It can take the shape of articles, movies, podcasts, or any other type of content designed to draw in and hold an audience. It may be done through websites, emails, newsletters, etc.

By creating SEO-friendly material and assisting in raising brand recognition, content marketing is another natural strategy to increase traffic. The fact that firms with blogs receive 67% more leads than other businesses may be used as evidence that content marketing, when done effectively, produces excellent outcomes. Brands may communicate their ideas and vision for their products and generate leads by using content marketing.Businesses that blog receive 67% more leads than competing businesses.

Whatever marketing strategies you choose, content marketing should be an integral component of your workflow rather than a stand-alone strategy. All marketing strategies include high-quality content. But keep in mind that having a written content marketing plan is very necessary for success. The three phases of content marketing are as follows:

Your content should be centered on the primary issues of your audience at the beginning of the sales process. You have the highest opportunity of connecting with them via writing about their problems, obstacles, and inquiries. Save your selling for the contemplation and closing stages; instructional and how-to content should be used during the awareness stage.

Content should combine marketing with useful information. The reader should learn about the features or functions and how different features meet their demands. Of course, the focus of your writing should be on the services that your company provides. When a potential customer is about to make a purchase, content marketing is crucial. You may concentrate on sales at this point as long as you keep emphasizing why you're the greatest option rather than just how excellent your services or products are. Your knowledge, experience, and the unique advantages of what you sell should be the main points of your message.

Online advertising is a type of marketing that uses the Internet as a distribution channel to drive visitors to websites and send advertising messages to the appropriate target audience. Online advertising aims to define markets through special and practical uses.

Online advertising has grown exponentially since the early 1990s and is now considered normal practice for both small and large businesses. The speedy marketing of product information without regard to geography is a significant benefit of internet advertising.

Search engine results pages, social networking sites, email spam, online classified advertisements, pop-ups, contextual adverts, and spyware are all examples of online advertising.

One of the following frequently used methods is used to acquire online advertisements:

Cost per Thousand (CPM): Advertisers are charged when certain audiences see their messages.

Cost per Click (CPC): When a user clicks on an advertisement, advertisers get charged.

Cost per Action (CPA): Only when a certain action (often a purchase) is carried out do advertisers pay.

The most effective method for reaching the target demographic and raising brand recognition is thought to be online advertising. Numerous tools have been made available by platforms like Facebook and Google to assist brands in creating their advertising and reaching their target audiences. Additionally, unlike conventional marketing, online advertising has given firms the chance to monitor and assess reach.

Nowadays, it's simple for advertisers to take use of their reach and promote their products on the majority of social media platforms. They also come with strong analytics tools for evaluating the effectiveness of the investment.

you might start to think about social media advertising. This can involve a boosted tweet or post, a promotion of user-generated content, or perhaps a full campaign that is disseminated across numerous social networks.

Content promotion
Its main objective is to improve a website's organic traffic through SEO; but, once a plan and content are in place, you may expand the content's reach and engagement by paying for it to appear on related websites. The ROI of content marketing may be increased with paid advertising. Without advertising, the expenses of manufacturing may frequently exceed the potential return.

Internet advertising
By paying to appear on search engines like Google, search engine marketing aims to make your website more visible on the search engine results pages (SERP).
It should not be confused with SEO (search engine optimization), which is the practice of getting as high up in the search results as you can without spending money to do so.

Online advertising on properly chosen websites that support your brand positioning is one of the safest methods. This implies that instead of being on websites selected by a third-party platform, you will always appear on websites that you truly wish to be on.

Mobile Marketing

Given how many of us use our smartphones for a significant portion of the day, it seems to sense that businesses are turning to mobile advertising to connect with consumers. Advertising using mobile applications, push notifications, SMS/text messaging, and MMS are just a few examples of mobile-specific marketing strategies.

Email marketing is a potent marketing channel that uses email to advertise the goods or services your company offers. Email marketing is a type of direct marketing as well as digital marketing.

Through various forms of marketing emails, it may also be extremely important to your lead generation, brand recognition, relationship-building, and customer engagement strategies.Email marketing may help you establish a connection with your audience and increase traffic to your blog, social media accounts, and other websites you want people to visit. To ensure that consumers are only receiving the content they wish to view, you may even segment your emails and target users based on demographics.

Here are some starting points for your email marketing strategy.

- Using email marketing software that can be set up to send emails effortlessly, you can also do A/B tests on a subject line or call to action to determine the best-performing content.

- You might now be asking how, in the first place, you create an audience of individuals to send emails to as part of your internet marketing activities. This is your only option.
- Sending to bought lists is banned because many email marketing organizations have strong, permission-based policies surrounding email addresses. Instead, focus on employing lead magnets to persuade them to opt in to get messages from you. If clients join your email list, you may give them a discount on their initial purchases.

- When sending automated emails, be careful to abide by all applicable local laws and legal requirements. such as the General Data Protection Regulation (GDPR) in the European Union or the Canadian Anti-Spam Law (CASL) in the United States for the handling of personal information.
- Use email to communicate with your clients. Email is a fantastic marketing tool, but it also has additional benefits for your company. Consider interrupting your usual marketing material every now and then to send out surveys, thank consumers for their business, check in with clients who left their shopping carts unattended, or simply say hi.

- Don't misuse someone else's confidence after they've given you their email address. Sending too many emails to your audience will make them unsubscribe completely or lose interest. Send them communications that are pertinent and interesting.

Each of your consumers probably receives 121 emails every day. Therefore, if you don't take the time to plan, your emails will either end up in spam folders or be lost in clogged inboxes.

You may learn to create an email strategy that works and send emails that recipients want to read. You only require a plan.

- Identify your target market.
- Specify your objectives.
- Get participants to register
- Choose a campaign type.
- Set up the emails.
- Analyze your outcomes

Once your email marketing plan is established, you may want to have a look at the following advice to properly format your emails and increase traffic. A meaningful offer should be the destination of your call-to-action, which should be distinct from the rest of the email.

Pay-Per-Click (PPC) (PPC)

PPC, short for "pay-per-click," is an online marketing strategy in which advertisers are charged a fee each time one of their adverts is clicked. It essentially involves paying for visitors to your website rather than attempting to "earn" them naturally.

One of the most well-liked PPC strategies is search engine marketing. When someone searches for a term that is related to their product or service, it enables marketers to bid for ad placement in the search engine's sponsored links.

Building a successful PPC campaign involves many steps. Choosing the appropriate keywords, conducting thorough keyword research, grouping those keywords into structured campaigns and ad groups, and creating PPC landing pages that are conversion-focused. Search engines provide discounts on ad clicks to marketers that can develop relevant, intelligently focused pay-per-click campaigns. Because Google will charge you less per click if your advertising and landing pages are helpful and enjoyable to customers, your company will make more money.It would be unjust to exclude Google advertisements whenever we discuss pay-per-click. , if we go where we if add. ad. ad. adds Let's get to know it a bit better.

Just what are Google Ads?
Google processes 63,000 searches per second, and Google advertising is often displayed on search results pages. Google advertisements are purchased by companies and maybe a very efficient method to get qualified, relevant traffic to your website at the exact time when people are looking for the kinds of goods or services your company provides.
Google sells advertisements that can be seen in search results on google.com using Google Ads or on other websites using the Display Network and Google's AdSense program.

The world's most widely used PPC advertising platform is Google Ads. On Google's search engine and other Google sites, businesses may generate advertising using the Ads platform.

Users that use Google Ads on a pay-per-click basis place bids on keywords and get charged for each click on their adverts. Google selects a group of winners to fill the priceless ad space on its search results page each time a search is performed by sifting through the pool of Ads advertisers.

The "winners" are determined by a number of variables, such as the standard and appropriateness of the keywords and ad campaigns, as well as the volume of keyword bids. Because Google is the most widely used search engine and receives a lot of traffic, it provides the most ad impressions and clicks, making PPC marketing with Google Ads particularly advantageous.

The keywords and match types you choose will determine how frequently your PPC advertisements show. Your PPC advertising campaign's success will depend on a variety of elements, but by putting your attention on the following, you may accomplish a lot:

Create relevant PPC keyword lists, compact keyword groupings, and appropriate ad copy to ensure your keywords are relevant.

Landing Page Quality: Developing optimized landing pages with compelling, pertinent content and a strong call-to-action that are suited to certain search queries.

The quality and relevancy of your keywords, landing sites, and PPC ads are evaluated by Google using a system called quality score. Advertisers who have higher Quality Scores receive more ad clicks at less prices.

Creative
It's important to have enticing ad language, and if you're advertising on the display network, you can utilize a tool like our free Smart Advertisements Creator to make ads of the designer caliber that will compel clicks.
You may overlook hundreds of thousands of useful, long-tail, affordable, and highly relevant phrases that might increase traffic to your website if you simply conduct keyword research once when you establish your first campaign.

Select the following keywords: Relevant Exhaustive Expansive
You must routinely manage your new campaigns after you've built them to ensure their effectiveness. In actuality, one of the strongest indicators of account performance is consistent account activity.

Mobile Advertising
Recent statistics indicate that 40% of internet time is used on mobile devices. The mobile age is already here.

You're already falling behind if you don't have any sort of mobile marketing plan in place. The technique of selling your company to consumers via mobile devices is known as mobile marketing.

When used effectively, mobile marketing gives clients and potential customers who use smartphones individualized, time- and location-sensitive information so they can receive what they need just while they need it, even when they're on the go.

Ads for mobile marketing are those that show up on tablets, smartphones, or other mobile devices. As numerous social media platforms, websites, and mobile applications provide their own distinctive and personalized mobile advertisement alternatives, mobile marketing ad formats, customization, and designs might differ.

But keep in mind that nothing succeeds without a solid marketing plan in place, and mobile marketing is no exception.

Because of the times we live in, your company needs a mobile marketing plan just as it does a computer and wifi. It's impossible to ignore the development of mobile when you take a stroll through any large city and see several people with their faces glued to their smartphones.

You need to be aware of the many forms of mobile marketing techniques.

Marketing Through Apps

Mobile applications are used in this form of mobile advertising. Despite the fact that 80% of mobile time is spent using apps, you don't need to develop your own to participate. Advertisers may generate mobile advertising that displays within third-party mobile apps with the aid of services like Google AdMob.

Advertisers are able to design advertising on Facebook's mobile application as well. Users frequently are unaware that they are viewing advertisements since Facebook's mobile Promoted Post ads blend in so well with the news stream.

Marketing Based on Location

Mobile advertising that is shown depending on a user's location in relation to a certain place or company is known as location-based mobile ads. For instance, some mobile marketers may only want their advertising to show up when consumers are within a mile of their place of business.

SMS Text offers are sent to users who have provided their phone numbers as part of SMS marketing. This is viewed as rather dated.

Smartphone Search Ads

These are standard mobile Google search advertisements that frequently include additional add-on extensions like click-to-call or maps.

Image Ads on Mobile

an an an an as an an an an a

Even though mobile marketing might be intimidating, you can make it simple by remembering these few pointers.

(I) Social Strategies

A new company's launch is usually a challenging yet rewarding process. Your motivation and enthusiasm are at an all-time high as you strive to maximize your company. As a consequence, in order to make the process as effective and efficient as possible, it is crucial to have a strong strategy in place for everything. Today, we'll discuss the fundamental components of your social media strategy by going through 5 quick-start tactics. Continue to read!
Let's begin.
Today, we'll discuss 5 methods to aid you in taking the initial steps.

- Make a business strategy for social media.
- The significance of selecting the appropriate social media channels for you
- Consult a calendar of events for ideas.
- Make a publication schedule.
- Start the relationship

Following these instructions, you'll learn about 5 crucial business-boosting methods!

Make a business strategy for social media.

Making a decision on the direction you want to take your company's social media page is the first step in developing a successful one. Think about the social media aim, business objectives. Below are some recommendations for you:
- Business purpose:
- Expand your brand
- Convert clients into promoters
- Drive sales and leads
- Increase client loyalty

The goal for social media:
- Awareness
- Conversions to Engagement
- Consumption metrics, Shares, Followers, etc.

It's time to construct a profile once you've determined what you hope to achieve with your business's social media presence. There is a certain sort of user for each channel. If you want to optimize your content, it is essential to comprehend how this audience varies from one another. Investigating these sites' demographics is relevant in this context.

(II) Facebook And Instagram Marketing

You may establish adverts on social media platforms to reach your target market. Additionally, they help you increase conversions, online revenues, and brand awareness. Additionally, Facebook provides a range of chances for lead creation, brand marketing, and campaign advertising.

How Can We Create A Facebook Ad Campaign That Is Successful?

Statistics show that Facebook is a lead generation powerhouse. Over 7 million marketers utilized it to generate leads.

Additionally, 26% of Facebook users who clicked on advertising completed a transaction. Businesses focused their efforts on finding new clients from this source as a consequence.

How Can a Facebook Advertising Campaign Attract Customers?

It might be difficult to use Facebook advertisements to draw in customers, especially if you are unfamiliar with the site. You must choose the right CTA type, carry out ongoing A/B testing, choose the right audience, write compelling descriptions, etc.

Launching the advertising campaign is solely your duty, even though you may use a professional writing services review website like Best Writers Online to help you create quality content for Facebook advertisements.

If you have never utilized Facebook advertisements before, the process could first appear challenging to you. However, once you understand how it works,

- You will see how easy everything is.
- Provide issues with answers.

- Make your Facebook advertisements more about your clients than about your business.
- Finding solutions to their difficulties is the greatest method to deal with them.

One of the most crucial strategies to draw potential buyers to your adverts is to use high-quality material and information. Your advertisement needs to address problems and speak to your target market. Your article should offer a clear, simple answer to the client's "suffering" and follow the proper structure (i.e., his problem.). Making good content is a challenge for many individuals. Fortunately, you may get assistance with this process from websites that evaluate professional writing services, such as Writing Judge.

Run many campaigns concurrently.
It is advised that you don't fund a single campaign that will help you achieve your objective. Run three distinct campaigns instead, one for each funnel level (top, middle, and bottom).
The main purpose of your top-of-funnel advertisement should be to increase awareness and pinpoint your audience. To get the most out of your marketing budget and benefit from the public relations services, run several campaigns, each one targeted at a particular demographic. You may spread out the same amount of money across several campaigns while still spending it. You will be able to produce the best advertisement for your target market as a consequence.

Create the adverts on your own

You shouldn't let Facebook configure your advertisements for you since you are the only one who truly understands your target market, including all of its issues, demands, and advertising objectives.

Always customize your adverts yourself as a consequence.
Many companies make the mistake of letting Facebook tailor its advertisements to their convenience. But by doing so, companies forgo a fantastic chance to favorably build up advertisements precisely for their target age range. When starting your next Facebook campaign, bear in mind that age is frequently a deciding factor in hobbies, activities, and health care.
Utilize advertisements wisely for possible clients.
One of the finest methods to achieve this on Facebook is by using Lead Ads. Facebook advertisements for prospects must be used effectively if you want to get a decent return on your investment. Make your suggestion as explicit as you can.

Without initially performing your research, you shouldn't immerse yourself in Facebook advertisements, especially prospective ads. Companies need to have a thorough understanding of both their target market and the goods and services they offer. The advertisement needs to stand out and appeal to consumers. For instance, if your advertisement targets customers who purchase food online from restaurants, you must specify where, how, and when the delivery is delivered. What options do customers have for restaurants? And how to coordinate the other aspects of collaboration while paying for the delivery.

When releasing advertising campaigns, it is crucial to have a clear understanding of what you have to offer. As a result, you have already eliminated clients that have no interest in doing business with you. At the same time, you draw in the proper clients who are already aware of how perfect your product is for them.

Watch videos

Observations show that video advertising gets 20% more views than picture ads, suggesting that firms should start spending money on videos to boost their social media marketing initiatives. Give potential customers a cause to click on your advertisement by offering a free download, such as a manual, checklist, quick guide, discount, or promotion. If they feel they will get anything from a lead, they will follow it!

KISS

KISS, which stands for "Keep It Simple, Stupid," is an acronym. This guideline is frequently applied in the design sector, but it may also be applied to Facebook advertisements. To improve the appearance of your adverts, simplify the chores.

Make Facebook advertising and lead forms as user-friendly as you can. Make sure they are as simple as you can. Facebook users like scrolling up and down through advertising while they travel, unwind, etc.

They don't have to be entirely focused on your adverts, though. As a result, the focus should be made on addressing the audience in a direct and straightforward manner.

Dynamic advertising is now available, allowing you to test and optimize advertisements for optimal performance using machine learning. To reach your target audience, you should constantly aim for the most appealing creative message.
Always have a unique messaging/PTC to address the issues of your audience, especially if you have various audiences or are at different phases of the funnel.
Avoid making things seem difficult.
Make sure your Facebook advertising is as simple and straightforward as you can.

Overanalyzing or overcomplicating the language is the most frequent error committed by newbies. For instance, using complicated language to make arguments that are utterly illogical. Use a straightforward and obvious call to action if you want users to click on your advertisement. There should be no question as to what your advertisement is selling. You will be more effective in luring this target consumer in if you are more explicit.

The process of getting leads from Facebook may be drawn-out and time-consuming. The quantity and quality of your prospects will significantly increase if you implement these recommendations into your marketing plan.

Instagram Marketing

Although difficult, Instagram marketing is competitive. Use this manual and our 18 suggestions to be successful in 2023 and beyond.

Instagram marketing is leveraging the platform to increase your brand's visibility, audience, leads, and sales. Instagram is a very efficient marketing channel for companies, business owners, and artists since it is the preferred social networking site for users between the ages of 16 and 34.

Marketing techniques for Instagram include:
Organic content: postings with pictures, videos, carousels Reels, Stories
Instagram advertising, such as Stories ads, Shopping ads, and more are considered paid content.

Steps for configuring Instagram for marketing
Here are the steps you should take if you're just getting started to make sure your business's Instagram account is successful.
Create an Instagram Business account.
A business account on Instagram is required to use the majority of the marketing advice presented here. You may either start a new one or convert your current Personal account; both options are free.

If you already have a Personal account, move on to Step 3.

Download Instagram first.
Only a mobile device may be used to register for an account.
Access it on iOS.
Access it on Android.
Create a Personal account in step two.
Tap open a brand-new account. Enter your email address, phone number, username, and password after following the on-screen instructions. You don't need to finish creating your profile just yet (more on how to optimize it later).

Switch your new account to a business one in step three.
Open the menu on your profile by going there. Select Switch to professional account at the bottom of the Settings page. To convert your account, choose the Business account type and then follow the on-screen instructions.

Get validated
Most businesses lack verification. According to research, just 0.87% of those with 1,000–5,000 followers are verified, compared to 73.4% of those with over a million followers. Even if you don't need the tiny blue checkmark to succeed on Instagram, having one might make you seem more credible and distinctive.

To submit an Instagram verification request:
1. Go to the menu in the app. Select Account, then Settings, and then Request Verification.

Fill out the form for source.

You'll get the response as an Instagram notice around a week after submitting the form. Instagram will never send you an email, request money, or get in touch with you in any other way.

You have 30 days to resubmit your verification request if it is denied. If it's accepted, congratulations and welcomes to the prestigious Instagram club.

Having enough third-party content to demonstrate your notoriety necessitating verification is the difficult aspect of being verified. In this comprehensive guide to being verified on Instagram, we go through advice for obtaining that supporting content.

Test out Instagram advertising Using advertisements to broaden your marketing plan may be quite effective. Instagram advertising can be launched in one of two ways:

The simple method amplifies a post

By selecting the Boost Post option, you may transform any current Instagram post into an advertisement. You must possess

Likes and related pages: This will broaden your target market beyond your current readership and include those that the algorithm deems to be comparable.

Make sure you adhere to Instagram Shopping standards in step one.

The merchant guidelines of Meta must be followed by brands using the shopping capabilities. Even if you're most likely doing everything right now, it's a wise idea to examine Meta's commerce policies before applying.

Sign up for Commerce Manager in step two.

You need to sign up for a Meta Commerce Manager account in order to start your Instagram Shop. You must have an Instagram Business or Creator account before you can join up using one of two methods:

Using your e-commerce website

You may step up your visual design if your website is powered by Shopify, Magento, WooCommerce, or one of the other main platforms.

Instagram is a visual social media site. Even if no one expects a small business to have the same resources as a megacorp, you still need to write pieces that capture people's attention and draw them in.

In addition to using a professional photographer, you absolutely should try:

buying stock photos that represent the complete spectrum of human experiences, such as Vice's Gender Spectrum Collection. To improve your look without spending a lot of money, use graphic templates. Use software like Adobe Express or hire a designer to create them.

Encourage your customers to post images or videos of your goods on social media. The authenticity of actual consumer images and tales cannot be beaten, even though not every photograph will be an Ansel Adams-caliber one.

With the Tagged tab, which displays all the posts in which other users have tagged you, Instagram makes this simple. There is a trick to make only the best of the best visible: allowing tagged photographs to receive manual approval.

You may thus choose user-generated material that matches your aesthetic rather than a disorganized mess.

Establish a brand look and feel

Having a style is important. Although your audience won't give you their money just because you look good, try to make your profile appear professional. Why? Because when someone sees one of your photos in their Instagram feed, they will immediately recognize it as coming from you without even needing to read the account name. They will identify your style.

That is branding in action. But don't let appearances get in the way.

Yes, having a distinctive appearance might help you draw in the target market you desire, but style without content is not a strategy. Instagram users, who make up 58%, said they like it when businesses offer real, unfiltered material.

Don't allow your material to be hindered by the worry that it isn't "beautiful" enough. Post it nonetheless.

Having a unique brand voice

Your brand voice is one thing that must always be on point, whether it is polished or not.
Everything you say carries your voice, including:
image captions
how you seem in videos

Make insightful Story highlights
Stories only last for 24 hours, but your highlights will always be available.
Highlights are excellent for conveying a lot of information rapidly in the style that is now preferred by most people:
Brief video under one minute long are preferred by 61% of Gen Zers and Millennials.
Additionally, including Stories highlights is a method to reuse your Story content so that it continues to be useful.
A temporary highlight could be added for a new product launch or event. Keep those that are always applicable, such as FAQs or purchase details.
Obtain the following for effective Stories highlights:
Clear, concise titles
Cover layouts that complement your brand
Only the very finest of your stuff was included.

Tools for Stories
Whether you have Commerce Manager set up or not, Instagram makes it simple to link to your goods or services and interact with your audience.

Tap the cheerful sticker icon to open the Stories toolbox, which is always expanding:
Don't forget to try:
You can quickly tag your items in Stories if you have an Instagram Shop. Users may tap a product's name to complete an in-app purchase.
Links are helpful for bringing visitors to any URL, but they are particularly helpful if you don't have an Instagram shop. You may still point external websites at your stuff.
Ask questions and receive timely advice.
Gift cards and more: Depending on the sort of account you have, users can order meal delivery or buy gift cards directly from a Story. With all the essential tools and capabilities, Hootsuite makes it simple to plan Instagram Stories in advance.

Update your knowledge of hashtags
Should I hashtag something? Is it more honorable to fight back against a sea of material or to endure the algorithm's highs and lows?
Per the Instagram post, a maximum of 30 hashtags are allowed. However, Utilizing more hashtags doesn't increase views. No more than 3-5 were advised per post by Instagram's official @creators account the previous year.
2023, how about it?
I conducted a random test on my account this week.

Our comprehensive guide to going live on Instagram includes instructions and suggestions you can use right away.

Join forces with influencers

In 2023, influencer marketing is still going strong and is expected to continue expanding. Influencer marketing generated $13.8 billion USD in revenue in 2021 alone. Your staff is your most significant influence; don't neglect them. Introducing an employee advocacy program may increase team morale and earnings by 23%. Win-win.

Hold competitions and giveaways

What does society enjoy? Free gifts!

How soon do they need it? Every time!

The oldest methods for using Instagram are frequently the most effective. You can get a ton of user-generated material and increase your organic reach by holding contests.

The cost of contests is not necessary. Users who like and comment on your post can enter a basic lottery for free goods, or you can collaborate with another business in your sector to divide the cost of a larger prize package. Discover innovative Instagram contest ideas and a step-by-step guide on organizing freebies to get inspired.

(II) YouTube, TikTok And Twitter Marketing

YOUTUBE MARKETING

YouTube is the second-largest social media site in the world, with over 2.5 billion active users each month. However, companies shouldn't only rely on YouTube's vast user base to convince them to utilize it in their marketing campaigns.

Consumers are increasingly using YouTube for pleasure, education, and product research. Your company may benefit from platform marketing by raising brand recognition, strengthening partnerships, improving SEO, and generating high-converting visitors.

The practice of advertising your company, product, or service on YouTube is known as YouTube marketing. YouTube is mostly used by marketers in three different ways:

Make unique videos: YouTube is primarily a platform for hosting videos. Success on the platform depends on publishing top-notch videos.

Associated with influencers Brands invested over $600 million in YouTube influencer marketing in 2021 for a reason. The platform is a great location to collaborate with artists and establish authority in your field.

70% of consumers claim to have purchased a product as a result of watching it on YouTube. Advertising on the site may produce significant benefits for your brand. Additionally, YouTube is the second-largest search engine in the world. However, getting ranked on the platform is difficult.

On YouTube, there are more than 5 billion videos, and 500 hours of new content are added every minute. Gaining visibility on YouTube requires a thorough understanding of the YouTube algorithm and careful video optimization.

What makes YouTube marketing so crucial? Consumers are 2x more likely to share videos than other sorts of material with their friends and family. The best location to use video material is on YouTube, where more than 1 billion hours of video are watched every day.

Your firm can profit greatly from YouTube marketing. Investing in YouTube should be your top priority for the reasons listed below:

Obtain a sizable audience
The user base of YouTube is enormous and quite engaged. You may generate a ton of traffic and visibility by collaborating with powerful artists in your area and constantly releasing high-quality content.
Even better, YouTube enables you to reach a global audience. More than 100 nations and 80 distinct languages have access to the portal. It's simple to produce tailored content for consumers throughout the

world thanks to features like automatically translated captions.

raise the prominence of searches

Although YouTube is a sizable search engine in and of itself, it also works wonders for increasing your exposure on Google. More than 94% of the videos in video carousels on Search Engine Results Pages (SERPs) currently originate from YouTube. You can select the best themes, match search intent, and optimize your films to rank higher on Google and YouTube by conducting keyword research on these platforms.

Amplify brand awareness

A wonderful area to raise brand awareness is YouTube. 90% of consumers use YouTube to research new businesses and goods, according to Google.

You may promote your company by releasing material such as product reviews, how-to videos, explainers, and video advertising. Additionally, employing strategies like visual branding and brand voice consistency may aid in making your brand memorable to your audience.

Build credibility and trust

The most reliable social media site for finding and buying things is YouTube. YouTube is a terrific place to start if you want to establish trust for your company. You may demonstrate how your product can address issues in a variety of ways, including through video testimonials, brand narratives, visual tutorials, hands-on evaluations, and live demos. Building trust with potential clients may also be achieved by collaborating with other producers in your area.

Boost traffic and sales
Marketers have a ton of options to sell things both within and externally through the platform thanks to YouTube's commerce capabilities including cards, end screens, channel stores, and tagged products.

Produce leads
Another useful tool for generating leads is YouTube. You may publish webinar teasers and online course trailers to entice people to join up in addition to employing tools like leads from advertisements.
You may also include links to lead magnets and landing sites in your video descriptions. To increase visibility, share your films on various websites and social media channels.

Make more income
While YouTube can support your current marketing plan, it can also generate more cash for your company on its own.
Channels that are eligible for the YouTube Partner Program can monetize their videos and earn money depending on views and interaction. To find out more about how you can make money on the network, see our post on YouTube monetization.
YouTube marketing ideas and techniques
Competitive YouTube marketing may be quite profitable if done correctly. It is not sufficient to just start a channel

and start posting videos. In order to achieve measurable success, brands must proactively plan, produce, and distribute content on the platform.

The tried-and-true best practices listed below can help you maximize YouTube marketing and use the platform to promote your brand.

Make your YouTube channel and rebrand it.

Setting up your channel, which will serve as your brand's "home" on the platform, is the first stage in YouTube marketing. You may upload videos, make playlists, reply to comments, examine analytics, and more here. Create a YouTube channel for your company by following this tutorial.

However, merely building a channel is insufficient. In order to develop consistency and create brand recognition, you must also brand it appropriately.

Make the following adjustments to your channel so that it complies with your branding style guide:

- A profile photo
- Banner picture
- Describe your channel societal ties
- The channel trailer
- Unique URL

Additionally, even if you need to optimize your video thumbnails, titles, and descriptions for SEO, make sure they are all consistent with your brand. Based on what works for you, you may establish a branded thumbnail template and stick to it for all subsequent thumbnails.

Are you trying to find a YouTube banner that won't cost you any extra money for design? Visit our free social media templates tool to obtain free YouTube banners for your channel right away.

Establish your YouTube audience.
Know the target audience for your videos before you begin to produce content.
Discover who makes up your target audience on YouTube as not all prospective buyers are using the platform.
- Do they have a gender?
- How old are they on average?
- What location are they in?

Create compelling films by taking your audience's interests into account as well.
- What type of media is your intended audience consuming right now?
- Which television stations do they watch?
- They're on YouTube for what purpose exactly?

Understand the issues, concerns, and objectives of your audience using a combination of social media market research, analytics, and social listening, particularly with regard to online video consumption. Create an audience personal to represent your target audience so you can keep them in mind when you make videos for your channel.

The YouTube algorithm also rewards videos with higher levels of interaction. To increase views and give your films a boost, promote them on other websites like social media and forums.Use cards and end screens to connect to your video from other videos on your channel. Finally, don't be shy about requesting likes, comments, and shares. You'll be shocked by how successful proactive outreach can be.

Use YouTube advertisements to attract certain audiences
You may increase your audience reach, increase website traffic, and target your audience with targeted messages by running YouTube ad campaigns.
Three ad kinds are supported by YouTube:
Before a video begins, there are a few brief, non-skippable advertisements called bumpers.

In-stream advertisements.
These appear during specific parts of your videos and may either be skipped or cannot be.Overlay ads are non-video advertisements that show up as text or banners above or below your videos.
When placing advertising on the platform, pay attention to your objectives. YouTube advertisements are supposed to support your organic approach rather than replace it. Additionally, views obtained through advertisements don't help with money from monetization.

Engage YouTube influencers as a partner
On the site, there are millions of creators who have thousands of devoted subscribers. Brands may collaborate with YouTubers who are experts in their

particular field to advertise their goods and services in unique ways.

Does it operate? 70% of marketers concur!

Here are some suggestions for promotions utilizing YouTube influencers:

- Box opening videos
- Product evaluations
- Tutorials and how-tos
- Day-to-day videos
- Giveaways and competitions

Prior to working with artists, establish a budget, and utilize influencer marketing tools to focus your search for the ideal brand partner. To speed up the process, communicate creative briefs with creators and set expectations upfront.

Plan ahead for product delivery, and regularly evaluate campaign success both during and after it concludes to make adjustments to your future approach.

Keep an eye on your YouTube metrics.

Monitoring YouTube analytics enables you to recognize your best (and worst) performing videos, comprehend the kind of material that connects with your audience and learn the particular elements that affect how well your videos perform.

In YouTube Studio, you may view the platform's built-in metrics. Keep track of statistics such as page visits, subscriptions, viewing time, audience retention, traffic sources, and devices.

Analyze the demographics and interests of the audience.
Understanding this enables success on the platform and the development of a successful long-term strategy. It also aids in concentrating resources where they are needed.

Tools for promoting on YouTube
All-in-one social media management tool:
Sprout Social
Sprout Social can help you improve your video strategy by giving you a set of tools for managing your YouTube channel. These consist of, but are not restricted to:

- Arranging for and posting videos on your channel
- Keeping track of video analytics and audience information
- Finding talks in your niche by practicing YouTube listening
- Managing your other social profiles and your YouTube comments in the Smart Inbox

And Sprout gives you access to a single dashboard from which you can manage all of your social network accounts. Connecting your accounts will simplify managing social media across all marketing platforms, including WhatsApp, Facebook, LinkedIn, TikTok, Twitter, and Instagram.

Canva's video branding tool and channel
Create branded graphics for your videos and channel with Canva, an online design tool. Utilize and modify

themes for banners, profile images, and thumbnails on YouTube. The application also allows you to use unique outros and intros for your videos.

Expand your company via YouTube marketing
One of the finest venues for businesses engaging in video marketing is YouTube. It provides advertisers with a fantastic opportunity to interact with their audiences thanks to its massive user base and extraordinarily high engagement rates.
Are you ready to start marketing on YouTube? Don't forget to monitor your development and adjust your plan as necessary. Check out our post on video engagement analytics to stay on top of the most significant YouTube performance indicators for your company.

TIKTOK MARKETING

By using TikTok marketing, you can be sure that everyone with a phone will hear about your company. For both Apple and Android-based smartphones, there is a free version of this software. There is no need to search for anything; simply scroll ahead to discover more material. There is a search engine accessible if you're seeking something specific.

Effortless Use
TikTok is a distinctive and user-friendly platform. Users only need to launch the app, visit the Discover tab, and they'll be presented with a limitless selection of films to

watch. Since you may get material from users you have not followed in addition to those you have, there is no need to choose who to follow.

Every TikTok user has unique tastes, and if they decide to sign up for an account, they may subscribe to the channels that offer their preferred material. Via doing this, you will be alerted whenever your favorite TikToker uploads any new material by a highlight.

The Target Market for TikTok

2017 saw the launch of TikTok by the Chinese startup ByteDance. Since then, it has grown to be a very well-known and frequently used social media app. TikTok, formerly known as Musical.ly, is essentially a centralized version of Twitter, Instagram, Vines, and Facebook.

The subject of the talk is marketing via this popular app. It's clear why this is a fantastic marketing tool for your company with over 1.5 billion consumers.

The target market for this special marketing strategy is mostly young people. This is ideal for a new company trying to attract plenty of customers! A pleasant domino effect will undoubtedly improve sales and income for your company since viewers will tell their friends and share the videos of what they saw. These additional viewers will then tell their friends and family about what they saw.

TikTok Marketing for Your Business

You may be wondering how you might leverage the TikTok platform, which is becoming more and more popular every day, to expand your company. Here are five strategies for utilizing TikTok to the benefit of your company:

In-feed Commercials
These interstitial advertisements provide businesses the chance to highlight their products. These skippable advertisements offer verifiable click-through rates, total views, and video viewing duration. They are also completely customizable.

Challenge Hashtags in Ads
This kind of advertisement may be found on the app's discovery tab. Users who click on the banner are sent to a page with details for the challenge, where they may take part in it. It channels the public's most current perceptions of your company and provides an opportunity for them to take part in something enjoyable while also promoting you.

Takeover ads for brands.
You may completely tailor your adverts on TikTok. To entice potential buyers, you will use GIFs, quick videos, or images in this kind of campaign. They will be taken immediately to your company's landing page by clicking on the advertisement.

Hashtag Contests
These were initially introduced on Twitter, but TikTok has carried on this entertaining method of product

promotion. This might be another fantastic marketing tool for both you and your company. #TikTokMarketing.

Participation of Users

This is unquestionably the easiest and most enjoyable approach to interacting with potential consumers. Users are encouraged to participate in this kind of marketing by giving their opinions about your company's services or products. In essence, your consumers write online reviews of your company and/or goods. These uplifting customer testimonials and videos demonstrate to potential consumers how delighted they were with their purchases.

TWITTER MARKETING

It's critical to advertising your company anywhere you can. Social media is one of the finest platforms for attracting customers' attention. Social media platforms like Facebook, LinkedIn, and Instagram may help you find individuals who are interested in your sector and provide you access to a sizable audience.

Another social media tool is Twitter, which has a character restriction of 280 and allows companies to communicate with their consumers about their opinions, promotions, and personalities.

Twitter marketing is a strategy used by companies to produce and distribute content to specific audiences, foster community interest in their brand, and ultimately drive sales. Twitter enables businesses to connect with a large global pool of prospective clients. In actuality, Twitter has more than 300 million active monthly users. It takes several steps to create a focused and successful Twitter marketing plan. Making buyer personas for your target clients is the first step. After that, it's a good idea to do Twitter research to learn more about your target audience's behavior and interests on the social media site.

It's time to start creating content for your chosen audience after you have a general understanding of their needs.
Nevertheless, pay attention to how people react to your tweets. You can refine and improve your plan and discover your brand voice by keeping track of how well your tweets work. Your Twitter strategy's success or failure can also be influenced by a number of little aspects. For instance, the timing of your posts might be just as crucial as the content itself. You must publish material when it will likely be seen by your target audience.

Principal advantages of Twitter marketing

Twitter marketing has a variety of advantages. You may use the platform to promote your business, interact and engage with potential clients, and stay informed about significant trends and advancements in your sector. Some of the major benefits of utilizing Twitter for marketing are listed below:

Brand awareness: Twitter assists in informing customers about your company's presence and its services.

Customer interaction.
Customers may contact you quickly and easily on Twitter. This fosters relationship-building for your company.
Twitter is a terrific method for directing consumers to your company website, which will increase website traffic.

Thought leadership.
Twitter enables you to engage in dialogue with your audience and express your points of view.
Customer research: Twitter offers a number of tools that may be used to examine the behavior and responses of your target market.

Sales for businesses.
Twitter is a terrific platform for promoting your goods and may boost revenue.
Create community: Twitter enables you to create a community of customers and backers for your enterprise.

many people are generally responding to your tweet?
Retweets:
- Are individuals retweeting your message on their personal Twitter profiles?
- How many followers are you getting from which of your tweets?

- In your tweet, you should add links to your company's website. Which links are the greatest at bringing visitors to your website?

Brand awareness.

Monitor how frequently Twitter users mention your company. Sales: How much of the traffic that is sent to your website results in transactions for your business?

Examine your objectives and change.

As you learn what works and what doesn't, you'll probably continually evaluate your strategy and update your material. Set objectives for your company's marketing strategy and what you hope to accomplish with Twitter. Make sure your objectives are precise and quantifiable. Connecting them to your KPIs is the most effective method to achieve this. Setting specific goals for your Twitter strategy may keep you focused and motivated by giving you something to strive towards. Goals can also act as a yardstick by which you can measure the success of your efforts.

Take the time to determine why you aren't progressing toward your objectives and revise your strategy if necessary. You might need to alter the kind of tweets you post, for instance. Compared to tweets with only text, tweets featuring photos and videos often receive far more interaction.

Start working on a better talent strategy now.

B2C vs. B2B variations in Twitter marketing approach for finding talent

The goal of both business-to-business (B2B) and business-to-consumer (B2C) marketing is to increase sales, although they do this in different ways. They also follow various schedules:

Building interest in a product or demonstrating the problem it can address for a consumer are typical B2C marketing strategies. The science underlying how a product works is often not of interest to most people. For instance, a user may come upon a blouse they like and decide to buy it by clicking a link to your online store.

The depth of B2B marketing is substantially greater. Business executives may be spending a significant amount of their money on a certain product, so they may want to learn as much as they can about it. B2B sales seldom occur instantly. Say your organization offers CRM (customer relationship management) software to companies. Your Twitter profile would serve both educational and promotional purposes, including demonstrating to companies what your product can achieve. A link to a white paper on your product can be included.

Optimum Twitter marketing techniques

We'll go over a few best practices and Twitter marketing pointers that can help you raise brand recognition and improve interaction in the sections that follow.

Examine Twitter.

Examine your own page's Twitter statistics to see how your postings are doing. Keep track of the number of individuals who are responding to your tweets.
- Are your hashtags effective and appropriate?
- Are you connecting with the people you want to?

You may change your content strategy going forward by identifying the tweets that are most effective. For instance, if you own a pet business, you could discover that tweets featuring attractive animals draw a lot of comments from people who love animals and want to share images and tales about their own pets.

maintain a unified brand voice

It's critical for businesses to identify their brand voice and adhere to it consistently. Your interpersonal style and personal expression are reflected in the brand language of your business.

Your brand voice may be witty, honest, or even caustic depending on the nature of your firm. A humorous tone, for instance, will draw customers eager to have a good time if you own a bar. A sentimental tone will draw folks who have a soft spot for animals if you manage an animal sanctuary.

Start by studying the brand voices of rivals in your market before creating your own. You could opt to develop a voice that is similar to other people or something completely different. As you see what resonates with consumers, your brand voice will evolve over time.

Check your brand's profile

Having your business verified on Twitter lets users know that you are a legitimate firm. Additionally, it can shield you from individuals attempting to pass as your company. You'll notice a blue checkmark next to your Twitter handle after your profile has been confirmed. However, Twitter doesn't only award blue checkmarks. To qualify, your profile must fulfill a number of standards. The following requirements must be met for your profile to be verified:

Your profile needs to be genuine.

You'll need to provide Twitter with a company website, a personal ID, and an official email address in order to establish your identity as the business. Your resume must be impressive. Twitter only validates users in well-known fields, such as business, entertainment, sports, politics, activism, and journalism. These profiles either need to be referenced in more than 95.95% of the profiles in your area or have follower numbers that are in the top .05% of profiles in their region. Your profile has to be active. You must have recently entered your account, and your profile must have a name and photo.

Visit the account settings on your Twitter profile to request verification.

You ought to come across a request for a verification option. You will be asked a few questions about your business on the form. In order to verify your identity, it will also request a few items from you, including your ID. Use hashtags properly.

The average increase in engagement (follows, replies, and retweets) for tweets with hashtags over those without is over 12%. With Twitter Analytics, you may discover some of the most well-liked hashtags for your sector.

Use ones that are distinctive and represent your company or certain campaigns you are doing. For instance, if you own an online record shop, you may tweet about a promotion for your business with the hashtags #VinylLife and #vintagevinyl. There can be no punctuation, symbols, or spaces in hashtags, which start with the "#" sign.

But be careful not to overuse hashtags in your tweets. One or two should be sufficient. Too many hashtags might cause users to lose focus on your topic. Additionally, it might make your tweets appear less authentic.

Locate reliable time management tools.
Successful Twitter users tweet frequently on behalf of their companies. Some businesses publish more than ten times every day. Posting when your audience is active on Twitter will ensure that you receive the best results from each tweet.

Depending on your business, there may be several ideal times to tweet. B2C corporation tweets, for instance Consider expanding to pertinent Twitter accounts.Twitter's ability to provide you with a simple way to interact with your audience is one of its finest features. A smart strategy to attract attention for your company is to engage in dialogues with your audience and respond to their remarks.

You may also get in touch with Twitter influencers to ask them to support your business. This will enable you to benefit from the significant following that certain influencers have. If a well-known influencer already follows you, you may be sure that they support your company or item. Use Twitter Lists to make sure you don't miss tweets from reporters, influencers, and potential customers that may help promote your company. You may use the feature to give your most influential followers' tweets more priority.

Review the tactics of the opposition

There are a few reasons to monitor the tweets of your competitors. It provides you with suggestions on how to engage your audience more. It also assists you in figuring out how to increase your market share.

Create a secret list of your rivals with Twitter Lists so you can follow all of their tweets. To determine how your business compares to the competition, conduct a SWOT analysis of your profile (Strengths, Weaknesses, Opportunities, and Threats).

Utilize social listening and trends to stay current. It's crucial to monitor what people are saying on Twitter about your company. Keep an eye on social interactions to determine whether individuals have favorable, unfavorable, or neutral opinions about your company. Monitoring talks about your business may be simple with the help of social listening solutions like Agorapulse and BuzzSumo. You may examine your reputation with the aid of these marketing tools to preserve or enhance it.

Keeping up with Twitter trends might assist you in growing. Before commenting on anything on a hot issue, though, be sure to complete your homework. The reputation of your business may be destroyed if an inappropriate tweet regarding a sensitive issue was sent by accident. To create tweets for the future, you may also plan for popular hashtags. Keep track of your research and approach

Creating content pillars is one method to arrange your Twitter strategy for documentation. The topics that your company will tweet about are grouped into Twitter content pillars. Your company goals should be the common thread throughout all of your content pillars.

As an illustration, if your development firm produces project management software, you might utilize the following business objectives as the foundation of your content:

- Inform the public about your products.
- Encourage customers to work more productively.
- Invite discussion regarding project management from your audience.

As you write your tweets, keep these principles in mind. A tweet intended to inspire users may include a motivational productivity remark from a well-known businessperson. Use Henry Ford's adage, "Nothing is very hard when you break it into tiny projects," as an example.

You may communicate with your audience consistently by using content pillars. You'll learn which tweets and content pillars your audience interacts with the most when you look back at your earlier postings. Your content pillars may change over time depending on how your audience reacts to them.

Great Twitter marketing tactics, to just a few
Many businesses are adept at using Twitter for marketing. We'll discuss a few companies that have made excellent use of the platform in the following sections.

A successful Twitter strategy is surprisingly difficult to develop. Making succinct tweets that will engage and draw a crowd requires a lot of effort. However, you may optimize a Twitter marketing campaign that will support the development of your brand if you conduct adequate research, provide pertinent material, assess your outcomes, and consistently update your approach. Upwork can link you with the top independent social media marketers if you're wanting to prevent social media blunders and maximize your company's Twitter visibility. They will be able to work with you to develop a Twitter marketing plan that promotes your brand personality while working for your company.

(III) Email And Website Marketing

The use of email in marketing campaigns to advertise a company's goods and services and to reward repeat business from clients. Customers on your email list may be informed about new goods, deals, and other services through email marketing. Educating your audience about the benefits of your brand or maintaining their interest in between transactions may also be a more subtle way to market. It may potentially fall somewhere in the middle. To obtain the most return on investment from your marketing program, Mailchimp can help you design, develop, and optimize your email marketing.

Email marketing is one of the most popular and successful marketing techniques available when you want to expand your brand or sell your products. In this article, we'll talk about how email marketing, specifically the use of promotional emails, may help you expand your business. We'll also offer some advice on how to launch a fruitful email marketing campaign.

Email marketing is a potent marketing channel that uses email to advertise the goods or services your company offers. Email marketing is a type of direct marketing as well as digital marketing. Incorporating it into your marketing automation initiatives may assist in informing your clients about your most recent products or offers. Through various forms of marketing emails, it may also be extremely important in your overall marketing strategy for lead generation, brand recognition, relationship development, and consumer engagement in between transactions.

Positive aspects of email marketing

Due to the fact that emails remain in the inbox until they are read, deleted, or archived, email has grown to be a very popular marketing tool for companies. Email marketing may help you establish a connection with your audience and increase traffic to your blog, social media accounts, and other websites you want people to visit. To ensure that consumers are only receiving the content they wish to view, you may even segment your emails and target users based on demographics.

By employing email marketing software that can also be set to simply send out emails, you can also use email marketing to do A/B tests on a subject line or call to action to determine the best-performing message. To learn more about the possibilities for email marketing, look at Mailchimp's email templates.

Issues with email marketing
There are certain negatives to email marketing, despite the fact that it appears like the ideal approach to connect with clients, find new prospects, and strengthen crucial business ties. The following are some important drawbacks of email marketing strategies.

Email marketing comes in a wide range of varieties. Each has a different function and employs a different strategy to interact with your audience. We'll examine a few of the various varieties so you can design the most effective email marketing plan for your business. Examples

Greeting emails
This style of email extends a warm welcome to clients and invites them to learn more about your offering. They frequently provide a trial or another perk. It serves to acquaint a prospective client with the company.

email newsletters
Email newsletters are quite popular, and they frequently feature new goods and services. They might also consist of articles, blogs, and client testimonials. Normally, there will be a call to action to encourage the reader to take action, such as reading a recent blog post or investigating a recent product.

emails for lead nurturing
Through a series of emails, this sort of email targets a certain audience to eventually convert them. Lead nurturing emails often target a group that is interested in a certain good or service and then increase their interest through subsequent emails that provide more information or pertinent incentives. Moving users from the contemplation stage to the purchase stage is the objective.

email confirmations
A confirmation email could be sent to people who have just joined up for emails or newsletters or made their first online transaction. By doing this, you can be confident that the prospect has gotten the information and is on the list to get more. These can include additional actions for users to take and are also a way to

inform users that their sign-up or purchase has been successful.

Personalized emails

A dedicated email is what you send when you only want to communicate with a specific segment of your email list. Recent purchases, inactive clients, new members, and other particular types of criteria might be used to compile its list.

Request emails

These emails frequently provide information about upcoming conferences, new product launches, and seminars. These emails are typically used by businesses to draw attention to and raise awareness of exceptional events when they occur.

marketing emails

These marketing emails are quite prevalent, frequently generic, and sent to a wide audience. They frequently serve to keep people informed and may even tease new goods and services.

email survey

One of a company's finest tools is feedback from consumers. These emails demonstrate to your consumers that you respect their feedback and are committed to developing experiences, products, or other offerings that they will find appealing. Businesses may also use the suggestions from these surveys to improve their products by incorporating them into their current lineup.

seasonal emails for marketing
Many businesses use the Christmas season and other special occasions to remind their clients and potential clients about impending deals and promotions. They frequently coincide with occasions like Mother's Day, Father's Day, Valentine's Day, and Christmas.

Advice on how to expand your email marketing list
However, how do you first create an audience of individuals to email as part of your internet marketing efforts? There is a handful, and they all revolve around serving your customers correctly while keeping in mind marketing best practices.

Purchase email.
Sending to bought lists is forbidden since many email marketing providers (like Mailchimp) have a rigorous, permission-based policy when it comes to email addresses. Instead, focus on employing lead magnets to persuade them to 1opt-in to get messages from you. When clients subscribe to your email list using a unique signup form, you might give them a discount on their initial purchases. You could also give new subscribers free shipping on their subsequent purchases, or you could give them the chance to win a gift when they subscribe to your list. Here are some additional pointers to aid with email list building.

Send only when necessary. Don't misuse someone else's confidence after they've given you their email address. Sending too many emails to your audience will make them unsubscribe completely or lose interest. They will remain loyal for a very long time if you concentrate on providing them with pertinent, interesting messages about the things they enjoy.

The email's subject line should entice the recipient to open and read it. Here is an illustration of some effective topic lines:
We are anticipating your order. 50% off today. Take a look at this brand-new item designed to make cleaning your house simpler.

Engaging your audience
Making valuable email campaigns is the greatest approach to engaging your audience. The reader may see if the email is valuable to them by looking at cost reductions, new goods, new services, and product advantages. They should continue reading. Email marketing is a fantastic strategy to keep your company at the forefront of prospects' and customers' minds so that they don't consider your rivals. All businesses want their campaigns to be successful and get customers to take action, which is what an effective email marketing campaign can achieve.

(III)Digital Marketing Sale Funnel

Sales funnel is the practice of examining the sequence of steps a user takes before achieving a certain objective, which is typically referred to as a conversion. You can see where users are losing interest and where there is resistance to conversion.

Key conclusions
The process of sales funnels is examining the series of several phases a user takes before converting. Websites often have four steps in their sales funnels: awareness, interest, desire, and action (the AIDA funnel). But depending on the kind of website or product, different steps of the sales funnel will apply. Sales funnels can be represented as funnels or bar charts. You may undertake sales funnel analysis at various degrees of detail with the aid of each visualization. Companies like Jitsi, Rappi and Blue Apron have all employed sales funnel analysis to increase retention, average order size, and conversion, respectively.

A funnel is a user's natural series of actions that they take to finish a task or convert. Consider them as stepping stones on a journey.
The practice of examining the customer journey to increase conversions is known as a sales funnel analysis. It's beneficial to detect any conversion-related friction so that teams may enhance the user experience and respond to consumer requests. Analyze the number of users who converted at each stage of the funnel.

Conversion rates over time may be viewed to help you understand how the sales funnel performs throughout the year for consumers that enter the funnel on a certain day.

Analyze the time it takes for a person to convert at each level of the funnel.

Frequency: The number of times a user completes a certain milestone action before converting.

Using the knowledge collected from funnel analysis for sales funnel management, you can:

- Identify the key areas for product enhancements to increase conversion.
- Find out which marketing channels get the best results.
- Recognize user behavior at each stage of the conversion process for users who convert and users who leave.

most typical steps of the sales funnel for products and websites

The AIDA funnel, which has four standard phases, is as follows:

Awareness

The user is made aware of your brand's presence.

Interest

The customer becomes curious about your brand and is willing to learn more.

Desire: The consumer displays a desire to purchase your brand after connecting it to a certain need.

The user takes action in the direction of conversion or purchase.

These four steps are generally represented by sales funnels for websites and products, however, the specific stages will vary depending on your sector. You may determine the stages of a sales funnel that are most relevant to the customer journey for your website or product by examining one. Here are four examples of sales funnels from various sectors.

online store sales funnel

Online retailers offer goods and services. The stages of a sales funnel for an e-commerce application or website include:
- Viewing a product advertisement
- Going to the webpage
- Doing a search for the item
- Putting the item in the shopping cart
- Buying anything

A sales funnel is similar to a kitchen funnel in that it has a wide top and a narrow bottom. It comprises parts that correspond to the steps people take to convert. It needs to be able to turn the data into a useful diagram that displays the number of users converting at each level of the funnel. The proportion of consumers taking the following actions steadily decreases as you proceed down the sales funnel.

A music-streaming app sales funnel example, with steps indicating conversion.

There are three sections in every sale funnel: top, middle, and bottom. The first section focuses on raising users' awareness of the product and teaching them about it. By giving more information about the product, the middle section aims to aid people in making educated choices. The last section discusses using conversion strategies to turn a user into a paying client.

The top sales funnel program
You may execute conversion funnel analysis more quickly with the use of funnel flow tools. You may do a sales funnel analysis using a variety of sales funnel tools, such as:
- Amplitude
- ClickFunnels
- GetResponse Autofunnel
- HubSpot Lead Management
- Kajabi
- Leadpages
- PlusThis
- Systeme.io
- Wishpond

(I) Building A Sale Funnel For Your Business

The steps someone takes to become a customer are outlined in a sales funnel. There are three components to it:

The marketing at the top of the funnel draws potential customers to your company (e.g., the advertising on your physical storefront, or the landing page of your website).

All the steps in your sales process that occur before the sale are included in the center of the funnel (e.g., people trying on clothing in your store, or website visitors reading about the benefits of your products).

The last purchase is made at the bottom of the funnel (e.g., customers paying for clothes at checkout, or website customers entering their credit card info to complete a purchase).

NOTE
Whether a person is brand loyal or has just learned about your company, a sales funnel identifies where they are in the purchase process.

How important a sales funnel is

The sales funnel illustrates the steps buyers will take to buy your good or service. You may better comprehend your sales funnel's operation and its weak points by analyzing it. Additionally, it will assist you in locating the gaps in the various stages of your sales funnel (i.e., where prospects drop out and do not convert into customers).

Knowing your sales funnel will enable you to control how prospects proceed through it and whether they make a purchase. As a result, you can invest in marketing initiatives that draw in more prospects, create more pertinent messaging for each stage of the sales funnel and increase the number of prospects who become paying customers. It will also give you insight into what customers are thinking and doing at each stage of the sales funnel.

NOTE
Grasp your clients' purchasing processes is crucial for identifying process gaps and investing in the most efficient marketing techniques. To do this, you must have a solid understanding of your sales funnel.

How to construct a sales funnel

Moving prospects from the initial point of contact to the point of sale requires the creation of a sales funnel. The prospect's position in the sales funnel may then be determined, along with the effectiveness of the funnel, by tracking the amount of behavior and engagement at each step.
A sales funnel may be made In a variety of ways, and several firms and sectors have their own kinds of sales funnels. To establish a sales funnel for your company, adhere to these steps:

1. Publish a landing page.

Prospect frequently has their first chance to learn about your company, its goods, and its services on the landing page. Users may click an advertisement or link on a social network website, download an e-book, or register for a webinar to get to your landing page.

Your landing page should concisely summarize your business and the special advantages of your good or service. Your sole chance to impress prospects may be on the landing page, so the text must be powerful and persuasive. In order to keep highlighting your value to the prospect, it should also contain a mechanism to get their contact details.

(I)Give something worthwhile.
You must deliver a benefit in exchange for a prospect's email address. For instance, you may provide a free e-book or whitepaper containing insightful and relevant information.

2.Keep the potential in mind.
Nurture the prospect with information that informs them about your product or service now that they have expressed enough interest to offer their email address. You should communicate with them frequently (once or twice per week), but not so frequently that the subject becomes monotonous or off-putting. Make that the information meets their primary requirements and dispels any possible objections.

3.Close the deal.

To complete the transaction, make your finest offer—one that the prospect will find difficult to reject. You may, for instance, provide a free trial, a product demonstration, or a unique coupon code.

Continue the procedure.
The prospect has either made a decision to purchase or not at this stage in the sales funnel. You should carry on the process of relationship development in any scenario. If the prospect ends up becoming a customer, keep the connection going by teaching them about your goods or services, interacting with them frequently to foster loyalty, and providing excellent service to keep them as valued clients. Send them frequent emails to keep in touch if the potential customer decides not to buy. Utilize several emails nurturing series to keep trying to convert them into clients.

4. Streamline your sales process.
Your work is never finished, even once you've established a sales funnel. You should always seek out methods to enhance and optimize your sales funnel and identify any areas where prospects are being lost. Pay attention to the sections in the sales funnel where prospects transition from one stage to the next.

Start at the very top of the funnel. Analyze the performance of each piece of content. With your original material, are you attracting enough potential customers? Your material should encourage potential customers to click the call to action (CTA). Rework that element or try something different if they are not doing that or if one piece of content is receiving fewer clicks on the CTA.

Analyze the landing page.
 The material (such as a blog post or Facebook ad) that directed the prospect to your landing page should be reflected in your offer and CTA. Do customers feel comfortable providing you with their contact details? Test each element of your landing page—including the headline, pictures, body content, and CTA—to determine what is and is not effective.
In the sales funnel's action step, test each offer. Compare the outcomes of several offers (e.g., free shipping versus discounts). How many purchases do your email nurturing programs and other marketing initiatives result in? If one offer performs much better than another, concentrate on using that offer to close prospects and consider how you can make it better.

Keep tabs on your client retention rates. Find out how frequently clients come back to buy your goods or services. Are customers purchasing more goods or services and returning frequently? Keep note of how frequently they recommend your business to others.

Note:
Create a landing page for your website and use digital content to direct users there to generate sales funnel leads. Next, get their contact information so you can stay in touch with them as they shop.

What distinguishes a sales funnel from a marketing funnel?

The marketing funnel ends when the sales funnel starts. By directing prospects from their initial engagement to the point when they are somewhat interested in knowing more about your products or services, the marketing funnel increases prospects' interest in your brand. The lead generation and nurturing processes are aided by the marketing funnel. The prospect enters the sales funnel after becoming familiar with your brand and leaves the marketing funnel.

(IV) Branding

By using components like a logo, design, mission statement, and a constant theme throughout all marketing communications, branding aims to give customers a strong, favorable impression of a business, its goods, or services. Effective branding enables businesses to stand out from the competition and develop a devoted consumer base.

Customers, therefore, anticipate consistent communication from you via email, your website, customer support, and all other business touchpoints. If you rebrand, you must update your styling online and offline as well as your logo. You make sure that your clients enjoy your omnichannel presence, and be sure to have a consistent brand.

Branding in-person may be significantly different from branding online since in-person considerations like product placement and props can affect how customers perceive your brand. Customers who shop in person have a more immersive brand experience than those who do so online since they can move about and pick up items. Of course, some aspects of branding are the same in-store and online. These contain logos and images that are recognizable.

The importance of branding

A distinctive brand may significantly affect your bottom line by offering you a competitive edge over your competitors and assisting you in acquiring and retaining clients at a far lesser cost. An established brand may be a vital asset in drawing clients and producing profit in eCommerce, where new businesses (and hence, new rivals), are popping up every day.

Your company still has a brand, whether you put time and effort into creating a memorable one or don't give it a second thought at all. It could, however, be very different from how you had envisioned being perceived.

You have the chance to shape your consumers' expectations and forge a special tie that transcends the buying-selling relationship by thoughtfully building your brand through stories, relationships, marketing messages, and visual assets.

Marketing is tactical, whereas good branding is strategic. You may start developing a marketing strategy that is focused on attaining those goals once you've established the higher objectives and precisely stated your brand promise.

Branding's Importance in eCommerce

Branding is a difficult process that needs methodical planning and calculated action. To avoid trying to match your online store with customer expectations by working backward, it is ideal to have your branding strategy planned out before you launch your online business. A powerful brand appeals to values that the target audience can easily relate to. A strong brand can act as a safety net to prevent a company from having to compete on price in an eCommerce store.

What steps should you take to create a brand for your online store? The crucial phases in eCommerce branding are as follows:

Recognize your target audience.
To communicate successfully, you must recognize the factors that affect your target audience and concentrate on utilizing them.
- What interests them?
- What inspires and draws them?
- What aspects of your brand do they enjoy?

Establish the brand persona.

A brand persona is the character of your company through which you will engage with customers. The information you can obtain about your target market will have a big impact on it.

- What voice pitch is appropriate for this audience?
- Which language will have the biggest impact?
- What pictures will catch their interest?
- Clarify the promise of your brand. What is your firmest commitment to your customers?
- How will your goods and services improve their quality of life?
- How will you fulfill your promise? Transparency is one of a brand's most appealing traits, according to 66% of customers.

Make your graphic assets better.

The visual experience is crucial since online customers do not have the pleasure of touching and experiencing the things they purchase. The front-facing components of a brand's visual assets include the website design, fonts and typography, color scheme, logo, and advertisement designs, as well as the package and unpacking experience you develop. It's a potent branding tool that performs at its best when each of the numerous moving pieces is consistent and functions as a whole. According to research, having a distinctive trademark hue would enhance brand recognition among consumers by 80%.

Improve the client experience.
Even if you have limited influence over how your consumers will eventually perceive your brand, you should make every effort to ensure that every contact and interaction you have with them is consistent with your brand promise and adheres to your brand rules. According to 69% of consumers, "understanding them" is the most crucial thing that companies can do to enhance their experience. This will include everything, including your shipping and return procedures, email marketing messages, and more.
loyal clients

Keep in mind to give back.
Saying "thank you" to your devoted clients might help to improve the perception of your business. Offer periodic freebies, discounts, or unique loyalty programs as a way to express your thanks. It's a guaranteed approach to creating enduring connections with your clients and personalizing your company's image.

(1) Increase Brand Awareness

The method that customers know and remember your company is through brand awareness. More consumers will be familiar with your logo, messaging, and products the more brand recognition you have.
Is brand recognition a marketing tactic?

Although this term is wide, brand awareness is also. It's a catch-all phrase describing how knowledgeable and attentive consumers are to what your business has to offer.

Customers are more inclined to purchase from your company than, for example, a competitor's firm that they are less familiar with since they already know your brand.

It's common to think of brand awareness as the top of the marketing funnel. You may reach a large audience of prospective customers by raising brand awareness. Leads may then be directed from there onto the research and decision-making stages, and ultimately the purchasing stage.

It's no secret that people today spend a lot of time online—more than six hours each day—so if you're trying to build brand recognition, the internet is a place you shouldn't ignore.

Take advantage of all the new awareness opportunities already accessible in the digital world as well as those that may emerge in the future by getting in front of customers where they are.

How to Boost Brand Recognition

After learning how to develop a brand awareness plan, you'll want to know how to raise and improve brand awareness.

These strategies fit in there:

Put native advertising to use

One of the best strategies for raising brand recognition and attracting new consumers is to use native advertising. Native advertisements let you target people where they're already reading and interacting since they seamlessly blend into their surrounding content and borrow credibility from their host publishing sites.

Here are our top suggestions for establishing a brand.

Referral initiatives
When users are certain they will receive an extra benefit, they will readily tell others about your product or service. A wonderful illustration of how clever referral systems can grow and hack a firm is Dropbox. For each friend they suggest, Dropbox provides current customers 500 MB of additional storage space (up to 16 GB). This referral scheme helped spread the word about Dropbox while it was still a startup, which resulted in a ton of sign-ups and allowed Dropbox to forego many advertising expenses.

Dazzling guest content
Creating really helpful, gorgeous-looking material that other bloggers will want to share is another fantastic approach to promoting your company online. Despite what some people may tell you, guest writing is still a strong technique to establish yourself as an authority in your field.
However, generic material won't cut it; you must be posting high-quality content as a guest. By producing

engaging content, you may reach new audiences and leave a lasting impact.

Infographics are a vibrant and colorful method to present eye-catching marketing facts and data. These powerful pieces of content are excellent for thought leadership and brand development since they are frequently shared widely.
Look at the infographic WordStream created earlier this year; it received a ton of social media shares and beneficial connections.

Credit-based freemium
Many fantastic online goods provide customers the choice to upgrade to the premium version, which enables them to remove the mark or replace it with their own brand, or to utilize the free version, which comes with a watermark or credit line. Even if many people will choose the free version, they will still spread the word about your business to other users. When new customers notice your product, some of them will choose the premium version! Offering a freemium product allows you to expand your audience, develop your brand, and attract paying consumers.

Local collaborations
Participating in local relationships is a fantastic brand-building tactic (this is tremendously important for local-oriented businesses, but can be applied to other businesses as well). Hold join intro seminars or festivals in collaboration with other neighborhood businesses.

Contribute to charitable causes and sponsor regional sports teams. Your brand will benefit greatly from being promoted at festivals and events.

Car decals

Getting a car wrap is a time-tested traditional method for establishing your brand! Customized artwork known as car wraps may completely around your vehicle (don't worry, you can still see out the windows)! They may draw a lot of attention, and they're a terrific method to make sure that your brand is being recognized more widely wherever you go. Wrap your own automobile or even the one you use for work!

Freebies

Free things are always a hit! Put your company name on koozies, pencils, Frisbees, and other products before giving them out at neighborhood festivals.

Facebook contests

Run a contest on social media where participants submit a photo or video and other users vote for their favorites. To increase the number of votes, contestants will spread the link among their social networks, which will increase brand recognition.

Social concern

Attempting to engage in active social media marketing on every social network would be futile given how many there are. Do not be afraid to focus most of your efforts on a few sites if your company is best suited to a certain network. For instance, photo-centric websites may emphasize Pinterest and Instagram. While small firms in creative sectors (like craft marketing) can succeed on Instagram, B2B enterprises frequently do better on Twitter. Recognize your audience's preferred networks and concentrate on them. Even while you won't want to completely stop using the other social media platforms, focus your efforts on what you are sure will succeed. Uncertain about your core network? Analyze your statistics to determine the source of your referral traffic.

Publishing on LinkedIn
Guest posting has previously been briefly discussed, but there are additional ways to get your name out there and be published. All users may now directly publish content to LinkedIn using the publishing tool, according to LinkedIn. Your posts may appear in many people's LinkedIn home streams if they receive enough attention. Additionally, adding posts to your LinkedIn profile assists in establishing you as a thought leader. Of course, you may also create a blog for your business and post there; just be sure to share and advertise your entries when they are published.

Seasoned storytelling
Want your brand to stand out? Start with a compelling tale. Users won't quickly forget your name if you can write emotionally stirring, captivating stories that connect with them on a deep level. Here is some advice on how to begin a tale.

Different personality
Giving your company a unique, engaging brand identity is a certain method to raise brand recognition. Being outrageous can increase brand recognition if you operate in a field where a little personality or humor is acceptable.
Examples of notable companies that use humor and comedy to promote their brands include Old Spice, Poopouri, and Dollar Shave Club.

These humorous commercials not only made an impression on viewers, but they also went viral, were shared online, and increased sales.

Podcasts
A fantastic strategy to establish your brand and network with people in your profession is to launch your own industry podcast where you interview industry leaders. Some fields, like marketing, already have a sizable number of podcasts, making it difficult for a newcomer to compete. (A couple of our favorite marketing podcasts are included here.)
However, you may quickly become well-known in specialized fields where there isn't much noise on the radio. Try podcast advertising as well!

Campaigns for remarketing
Remarketing is an effective tactic for raising current brand recognition. Why? Remarketing entails displaying advertisements to website visitors who browsed but did

not convert. Remarketing advertisements are posted on websites your client's visit all over the internet. They will soon come across your company everywhere, including on their favorite sites and while purchasing online, etc. This creates the false impression that your brand is much bigger than it actually is (and has a much higher advertising budget). Additionally, it's a fantastic strategy to raise your conversion rate.

Paid social media marketing
As organic social media marketing becomes more and more challenging, more companies are turning to paid social media advertising. Facebook and Twitter advertising are reasonably priced and aid in increasing business awareness on social media. Even if consumers don't convert right away, every additional bit of familiarity matters when they are ultimately ready to make a purchase.

Controversy
Being controversial is one method to get your business recognized, yet this tactic isn't for everyone. Take a controversial stand on a pressing industry issue, and you can find yourself drawing a lot of attention.

www.ingramcontent.com/pod-product-compliance
Lightning Source LLC
Chambersburg PA
CBHW052356220526
45465CB00003BB/1128